Quilts & Coverlets

THE BEAMISH COLLECTIONS

QUILTS & COVERLETS

THE BEAMISH COLLECTIONS

Rosemary E Allan

First published in 2007 by

Beamish,
The North of England Open Air
Museum

Beamish Museum Co.
Durham, DH9 ORG

Photography by
Rosemary E. Allan,
Justin Battong, Paul Castrey,
Duncan Davis and Peter Richardson.

Design by
Ian Brown Design Ltd.

Printed in England by Elanders

British Library Cataloguing in
Publication Data.

A catalogue record for this book is
available from the British Library.

ISBN 0-905054-11-3

CONTENTS

QUILTS &
COVERLETS

INTRODUCTION

'The quilting tradition is a skill from the living past which remains alive, enabling the quilter of today to create new beauty. It is in her hands, and in the hands of all who teach quilting, to see that it is passed on alive to the future.'

Traditional Quilting, Mavis FitzRandolph, 1954

BEAMISH, The North of England Open Air Museum, established in 1970, is now regarded as a treasure house of the North East of England. Its aim is to portray, on a superb 400 acre site, something of the life and work of northern people at two key points in their history, the 1820s and the 1913 period. Its collections, however, cover a much wider period and are now internationally renowned. The object collections are vast, concerning all aspects of social and domestic life, farming and rural life, industrial and town life, as well as transport all relating to the region.

The collection of North Country Quilts and Coverlets is truly magnificent and is recognised as one of the best and most extensive in the British Isles. Brought together from the counties of Northumberland and Durham, with examples from Cumberland, Westmorland and Yorkshire, the collection was assembled mainly between 1970 and the present day. It now consists of some 250 or so documented examples of the traditional craft, representative of a way of life, rather than of an art form. The history of quilting in the North reflects the social and cultural conditions in which the quilts were made, in a relatively isolated region, which had developed its own distinctive culture and identity.

The making of quilts and coverlets, whether for domestic, social, professional or community purposes, was not restricted to women. Indeed some of the best known quilters were men, who made their mark upon the tradition in a number of ways, though particularly in the piecing and designing of quilts, influencing much of the work that was to be produced by later generations.

Quilting and its evolution in the North of England could often be related to social class. Quilts were made for basic utilitarian reasons, for warmth in winter as well as to make the most of scraps of

material left over from the making of clothes and indeed from the old clothes themselves. They were also made by the lady of leisure, who had plenty of time to fill, in which to demonstrate her sewing and show off her embroidery skills in the production of fine ornamental work. Sometimes they were made to earn a livelihood for a miner's wife on hard times. Often they were a useful means of fundraising within a community or for a chapel building fund, at the same time providing great opportunities for a social get together and merrymaking. In later years so much pride was taken in producing these works of art, that they were entered for competitions in country shows.

The craft is often referred to as "Durham" quilting, however a more accurate description would be that of North Country quilting, as it was practised throughout the counties of Northumberland, Durham, Cumberland, Westmorland and Yorkshire, each region having its own characteristic and distinctive patterns.

Many quilts and coverlets have been passed down in families from one generation to the next, sometimes with stories attached as to maker and date. However, these can be inaccurate as memories fade with time and information is misremembered. At one time every house in the North of England would have had several bed quilts, each with its own history.

The dating of quilts and coverlets has always proved to be difficult, as a quilt could include fabrics dating anywhere between 1800 and 1900. Early examples were quite prized and were mentioned in inventories, wills and house sale particulars.

Details of patchwork coverlet with many of the paper patterns intact. Fabrics date between 1790 and 1820. (2001-10)

When bed quilts went out of fashion, they were often sold at auction, their history and provenance being lost forever. Now the museum curator must assess and re-evaluate each quilt and coverlet on its own merits and by examining the fabrics and style. The real treasures are those examples, which are signed and dated by the maker, but those are indeed a rarity.

The collection at Beamish is an important folk art survival in the British Isles.

This book is intended as a guide for those interested in the history of the northern region and in particular in the traditional craft of quilting, as well as being a catalogue of the Beamish collections. We hope to continue developing the collection, and in the not too distant future to have a permanent exhibition, where quilters and quilt enthusiasts will be able to appreciate this inspirational craft, preserving something of our fine North Country heritage for future generations.

Detail of unfinished patchwork, made by an elderly country woman from Allenheads about 1860-70. (1971-129)

QUILTING IN THE NORTH OF ENGLAND

Early History

The traditional craft of quilting has been practised from at least mediaeval times in England and may well be considered as one of the few examples of a genuine survival of 'folk art' in this country.

QUILTING consists primarily of three layers of material, an upper or top surface, which may be of plain, appliqué or patchwork material, a layer of wadding for warmth, and a bottom layer forming a sandwich, all three layers being held together by running stitches in a design, simple or elaborate known as quilting. In the North of England, the work is sewn by hand in a large quilting frame. A coverlet becomes a quilt when it has been sewn with quilting stitches through a layer of filler and a backing material. The filler or wadding is laid evenly distributed between the two covers, as opposed to the stuffed or corded quilting in which the wadding was used only for the design.

North Country quilts usually fall into one of three recognised categories: wholecloth, strippy, and patchwork and appliqué.

The word "quilt" comes from the old French "cuilte", which itself derives originally from the Latin "culcita", meaning a stuffed mattress or cushion. It is defined now as a bed coverlet made of padding enclosed between two layers of cloth and kept in place by lines of stitching.

THE ORIGINS of quilting are uncertain, but it has been practised from an early period throughout Europe as well as in Near and Middle Eastern countries. It would seem that quilted garments were worn more than 5000 years ago from evidence found in the Temple of Osiris at Abydos in Egypt.

In England, the use of the word can be traced back to the thirteenth century at least, when quilting was used in protective garments worn under or over armour or chain mail. Quilted clothing used as armour was both lighter in weight and less costly than plate armour to produce, and seemed to have been a satisfactory substitute. In the 14th and 15th centuries, the doublet became a fashionable item of clothing for outerwear. In mediaeval and later inventories, quilts are often mentioned, though they were very much the preserve of the upper classes.

Janet Rae in her book, **The Quilts of the British Isles** makes mention of a reference to early bed quilts in the North of England. The Very Rev. Daniel Rock, writing in 1876, in his work **Textile Fabrics**, talks about a quilt with the four Evangelists in the corners, on a bed in a priory dormitory in Durham in 1446. By this time quilts were looked upon as essential furnishings for beds and also for underlays. Although some inventories and references to quilts exist, we cannot be sure what these were like or indeed how old they were when recorded.

Another account can be found in the fifteenth century Account Rolls of the Priory of Durham (*Surtees Society Vol.9*).

'*Manerium de Wytton*
Item ij wiltez
Item iiij dormundez
Item j fedyrbed'   1465

Also for the same manor is listed

'*Item xxviij coverlettez diversorum colorum*
Item ij wyltez'   1472

A distinction was therefore being made at that date between coverlets and quilts, though both were considered to be of sufficient importance to be listed in inventories of the period. It may also be that quilts were being used under the mattress for warmth as well as over the mattress, as is suggested by the later accounts and inventory of Thomas Morton in 1581 (Surtees Society Vol. 38).

'*In the chamber*
On fayre wrought bedsted of waynscott 13s 4d
Downe bed in pawne 3L
On twylte under the bed 3s
On bolster 2s 6d'

The Haddon and Makepeace family tomb, in Heworth churchyard, Gateshead, takes the form of a four-poster bed with three children lying beneath what appears to be a wholecloth quilt. William, George and their sister died between 1711 and 1717, of an unknown cause. Their father was a master mason, and a man of sufficient means, enough to build such a memorial illustrating a quilt at a time when they would have been considered to be a fashionable item.

QUILTING was often combined with patchwork in both bed coverings and bed hangings. The earliest known example of English patchwork, which is at Levens Hall, near Kendal in Cumberland, is reputed to have been made in about 1708. The complete set of quilt and hangings is made up of pieces of Indian prints imported into the country at the end of the seventeenth century. The pieces were applied using a technique called "broderie perse". The quilting is stitched in an overall diamond pattern. Indian prints were much prized, though the 1770 ban on importing them, hindered their use but did not stop it completely.

The popularity of quilting in England generally reached its zenith in the seventeenth and eighteenth centuries, when it was used in fashionable costume of the period. This was largely a professional trade centred on London. Quilted materials for making up into clothing or quilts, were on sale in the London shops. Quilted suits of satin, doublet and breeches were worn by gentlemen, and elaborate quilted petticoats of silks and satins were an essential requisite for fashionable ladies, in the mid eighteenth century. A fine quilt, made by Elizabeth Grey of Southwick, for the marriage of her daughter Elizabeth to Charles, 1st Earl Grey of Howick, in 1762, is at Wallington Hall, Northumberland. The quilt is of fine white cotton and depicts a flowing design of tulips, leaves and feathers. The tulip had been introduced into Europe in the mid 16th century and was regarded as quite a status symbol amongst the upper classes.

A fine example of fashionable eighteenth century quilting being undertaken is illustrated in the painting A Conversation Piece : Family at Recreation by Isabelle Pinson dated 1781, (below) from the collection in The Bowes Museum, County Durham. This is an excellent example of quilting using a frame, albeit in a French setting.

The MSS Accounts book for the Surtees family of Mainsforth, Co. Durham lists : -

'August 8 1788 To glazing of patchwork 15-00' and
'May 12 1789 To Blue stuff quilted petticoat 6-9'.

In June the accounts list :-

'To 9yds of cotton for quilt lining 9-0' and
'July 22 Quilting a Bed Quilt 12-0
Cotton & thread 3-0' and
'Dec 17 Glazing a Quilt 1-2'.

The fashion in bed quilts continued throughout the late eighteenth and early nineteenth centuries, with patchwork taking precedence over wholecloth quilts. This was largely due to improvements in manufacturing processes brought about during the Industrial Revolution. Until 1733 the cloth weaver's productivity was limited by the speed with which he could throw the shuttle across the warp. Things changed dramatically with Henry Kay's invention of the flying shuttle, which speeded up production enormously. This was followed in 1769, by the spinning machines of Hargreaves and in 1786, by those of Arkright. The jenny, invented by Hargreaves, was a machine for spinning all types of woollen yarn. The early jennies were small and ideal for a cottage industry. Later the power loom and more advanced fabric printing techniques, transformed the entire textiles industry.

There was a preference for dramatic roller printed designs and bold striking colours in yellows, scarlets and blues in the fabric of the period from1790 up to the 1820s period.

Details of roller printed fabrics from coverlet (right).
(2001-10)

STRIPED FLORAL COTTONS were much in use from the 1790s, and later, between 1825 and 1835, the pillar print was a design much used and repeated. Block printed, mass-produced cotton panels were much in evidence at this time and provided useful centres for the framed or medallion quilt, as well as for chair backs.

Those quilts, which were made up to about 1835, were sewn in printed cotton, still a fashionable dress material. Quilts made after that date, reflect the changing fashions in printing techniques. Dress fabrics of cotton, remain the main source of material for patchwork quilts, although in the country areas, where wool was readily available, some quilters would have taken advantage of the numerous woollen mills to obtain their fabrics. The many posters printed by William Davison of Alnwick, in the early to mid 1800s, testify to the number of quilts in everyday use at this period.

During the late 18th and early 19th centuries, there was a gradual transition from the use of vegetable dyes to chemical dyes. The development of a very fast dye known as Turkey red, largely pioneered in the mills at New Lanark in Scotland, and readily available from the mid 19th century, had a huge impact on quilt making and design. Many wholecloth and strippy quilts were made using Turkey red, which was also popular for appliqué and patchwork.

Not only was there a huge choice of fabrics, by the mid nineteenth century, but the fabrics themselves were a fraction of the cost they had been, enabling ordinary working folk the opportunity to purchase and make clothing and furnishings of a much greater variety, often in imitation of the middle and upper classes of an earlier period. This availability of cheap fabric helped to popularise mosaic patchwork throughout Britain as a whole, whereas at the beginning of the century it had been the preserve of middle and upper class women, with sufficient money and time to undertake pieced coverlets, which were rarely quilted.

Many fabrics could be obtained from the local Co-op store, which provided the cotton wool wadding, bought in rolls, to be fluffed up, ready for the padding. The Co-op also sold the stamped quilt tops and travelled them around the more outlandish farms, where farmers' wives purchased them, to be used for special occasions.

The domestic craft of quilting survived, notably in the North and South West of England, as well as in parts of Wales and Scotland and Ireland, where the tradition ignored the world of fashion, and held its own in the cottages, farmhouses and colliery villages. Quilting tended to flourish in more isolated areas, its utilitarian qualities of warmth and economy, helping to keep it alive.

HOUSEHOLD FURNITURE

To be Sold by Auction,

FOR READY MONEY,

AT ALEMOUTH,

On THURSDAY the 13th day of October, 1831,

D. BUSBY, AUCTIONEER,

ALL THE

HOUSEHOLD FURNITURE

Lately belonging to Capt. Wake deceased,

Consisting of a Four-post Mahogany Bedstead, with Crimson Moreen Hangings, a Camp Bedstead, Put-up Bed, Feather Beds, Bolsters, and Pillows, Mattresses, Quilts, Blankets, Bed and Table Linen, Mahogany Tables, Mahogany Hair-seated Chairs, Wash-Stands, Looking-Glasses, Carpets, Tea Trays, Mahogany Chests of Drawers, China and Delf, with all the Kitchen Utensils, &c.   Sale to begin at 11 o'Clock in the Forenoon.

Davison, Printer, Alnwick.

TO BE

Sold by Auction.

FOR READY MONEY,

BY MR. D. BUSBY,

AT BELFORD,

On THURSDAY, the 11th of February, 1841,

ALL THE HOUSEHOLD

FURNITURE

BELONGING TO THE ASSIGNEES OF MR. JAMES THOMPSON,

Consisting of Bedsteads and Hangings, a Press Bed, Feather Beds, Blankets, Quilts, Counterpanes, Mahogany and other Tables, Cane-bottomed and other Chairs, a Mahogany Wardrobe, a Wardrobe and Desk, a Sofa with Chintz Cover, a Dressing Glass, a Carpet, Window Blinds, Fenders and Fire Irons, Candlesticks, Tea China and Crockery Ware, Tea Trays, Wine and Tumbler Glasses, Wash-Stands, Drawers, Meal Chest, Pots, Dishes, all the Kitchen Utensils, and a Saddle and Bridle.

The Sale to begin at half-past 10 o'Clock.

...bruary, 6th, 1841.

DAVISON, PRINTER, ALNWICK.

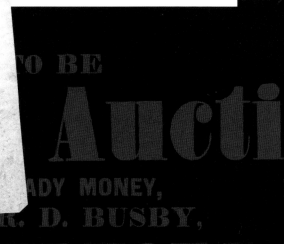

TO BE SOLD

BY AUCTION,

(FOR READY MONEY)

At the House of Mr Joseph Marsden, Innkeeper in Bamburgh, on Monday the 14th December instant, (by Order of the Sheriff of Northumberland.)

ALL the Household Furniture of the above Joseph Marsden, consisting of Four Post and Camp Beds, and Hangings with Window Curtains to Match, Goose-Feather Beds, Blankets, Quilts, and Counterpanes, Table and Bed Linen, Mahogany Tables and Chairs, Drawers and Desks, Room and Bedside Carpets, Looking Glasses, Table and Tea China, Fenders and Fire Irons, a good Cart Horse, Cart and Trappings, a Stack of well won Hay, a quantity of Potatoes, with all the Kitchen and Dairy Utensils.

The Sale to begin at 10 o'Clock.

Bamburgh, 9th December, 1812.

Davison, Printer, Alnwick.

Quilted Skirts and Petticoats

'Women with long heavy skirts which they lifted up to clear the dust or mud, with slender waists and bustles, making them look like an hour-glass, and two or three quilted petticoats which, when thoroughly wet, made walking a burden, would present a picture unbelievable, if not ridiculous to the youth of today.'

Weardale Memories and Traditions, written by John Lee in 1950, though referring to the late 1800s.

Elizabeth Bulmer in her quilted petticoat at Bardon Mill, Northumberland, c. 1910.

N MANY HOMES, quilting was essentially a thrift craft. As well as bed quilts and cradle covers, skirts and petticoats were quilted and worn by country people. Women field workers, known as bondagers, working on Northumbrian farmsteads, often wore quilted petticoats, which were made from heavier "thrift" woollen or homespun materials for warmth and economy.

*Here can be seen bondagers, some as young as ten years old,
near Alnwick, Northumberland in 1868. (5411)*

Some girls learnt to quilt petticoats before they graduated to bed quilts.

> *'Her twilted pettikit se fine*
> *Frae side te side a fathom stritchin'*
> *A' stitch'd wi' mony a fancied line*
> *Wad stan' itsel, and was bewitchin'.'*

Thomas Wilson wrote **The Pitman's Pay**, first published in 1826 and describes the craft:-

'The quilting of a petticoat in those days was a very important matter, equal to a week's visit from the tailor's. It was an awful sight to the male inmates of the house to see the quilting frame erected on the Monday morning, with many of the gossips in the vicinity set down to their highly important labour.

The whole attention of the mistress was given to these lady-stitchers; nothing else was properly attended to as long as this important labour continued. The best of creature comforts were provided for them; not omitting a drop of the bottle; for as they gave their labour without a fee or reward the choicest fare was expected. Amongst the improvements of our day, the poor man may thank his stars that quilted petticoats are no longer in fashion.' (1830).

From around 1800, quilted garments went rapidly out of use in fashionable circles, though, the quilted petticoat did of course continue in use, but not as a fashionable item of clothing.

William Morley Egglestone in his **John Askew, The Stanhope Violin Maker**, writing in 1914, though about an earlier period c.1845, *'long before the iron road, the railway, penetrated the quiet pent-up dales,'* describes the country pastimes: -

'In winter there were held at various houses on the hillsides or in the valley, gatherings known as merry-nights; quilting nights; tom-trot nights. All these were associated with fiddling and dancing'... *'Quilting nights were a gathering of young women, who went to help their host in the afternoon to make quilts then, after tea, their sweet hearts turned up and the night was finished with fiddling and dancing.'*

John Lee in his **Weardale Memories and Traditions**, of 1950, though again describing much earlier days, quotes *'should a quilt be in the making (and what pieces of art they were, both in design and work, especially the patchwork ones) with two or three quilters helping, then the talk would be a little harmless gossip on the ordinary doings of village life.'*

Quilted petticoats were still being worn in Yorkshire, on the farms of the Yorkshire Wolds, right up until the First World War. They were also worn by many of the fishermen's wives, living in fishing villages, along the North East coast, from Yorkshire right up to the Scottish borders.

Such petticoats were usually dark in colour and severely practical, with a limited amount of pattern. Lang Sall and Fat Bess, *(Sarah Cromarty and Bessie Morris)*, of Holy Island, were well known for carrying their fish to the mainland on the backs of their two mules and hawking it around the mainland villages in about 1885.

Not only were quilted petticoats popular in the fields of rural Northumberland, but also in the urban areas such as South Shields, where "Dorfy" writing between 1904 and 1914, remarked that *'It was not uncommon for women to wear three or more petticoats, one quilted, or of flannel, one of alpaca or silk moiré which rustled and swished, and one or several, white embroidery or lace trimmed with frills, - my aunt Polly wore at least four petticoats'.*

"Lang Sal and Fat Bess", fishwives from Holy Island, Northumberland. (5145)

Emigration

FROM THE 1860s to the 1920s, largely due to the demise of the lead mining industry, there was a considerable movement of families emigrating from the rural areas of the North East of England, to America, in search of work. A number of Weardale lead miners and their families went out to prospect for gold in the Klondike.

John Wilkinson (right) emigrated to the Klondike. Here he can be seen in 1897, counting his gold nuggets. (18,371)

A group of Weardale leadminers, (left), before emigration, c.1880. (15,295)

EMIGRATION—WHITE CROSS LINE. LONDON to NEW YORK. Reduced third-class fares, £5 via Antwerp. Departures Hull every Saturday, London every Monday.—Cecil Thompson & Co., 27, Leadenhall St., London.

Early settlers in New Amsterdam, New England, Virginia and the Carolinas, took with them the craft of quilting, from their old homes in Holland and England. It was natural that the emigrants would send patterns back to their relations, though it can never be proved that a certain pattern originated in a particular country. There was consequently a considerable exchange of patterns and designs on both sides of the Atlantic. It is said that Joe the Quilter from Warden in Northumberland, sent some of his work to America in the early 1800s. A number of well used patterns such as the *feather, twist, wineglass, rose* and *diamond* have been well used in both American and English quilts

Some excellent quilting was carried out in the nineteenth century and it was gradually becoming recognised as a fine handicraft in the British Isles as well as in America. The Arts and Crafts movement brought a consciousness to the craft and examples were being exhibited at the Great Exhibition in 1851. Improved industrial processes and transport as well as better availability and a wider choice of cheaper fabrics, brought about a renewed interest in quilting as a fine craft.

The post 1850s period saw American influences developing. A number of patchwork and appliqué quilts in vibrant colours were being produced, often using the pieced block construction in patterns traditionally favoured in the States, such as Robbing Peter to Pay Paul, Drunkard's Path and Feathered Star, Turkey Tracks, Princess Feather, and many more reflecting the life styles of the early settlers. The use of red and green on a white background was much favoured on both sides of the Atlantic. Dorothy Osler, in her article Across the Pond, in the **Quilter's Newsletter Magazine,** studies New World influences on Old World quilt traditions, and comments on the fact that some 40% of the British who emigrated to the United States, returned home, possibly bringing with them ready made quilt tops as well as new ideas. Quilt tops could also have been sent 'across the pond' as special gifts.

John Bee with his family, emigrating to Canada from Weardale in 1928. (10,230)

In about 1860-70, PHOEBE WATSON, of Low Burn Farm, Ireshopeburn, Weardale was making pieced and appliqué quilts, in styles very similar to some American quilts. A dressmaker recently widowed, she could not afford to pay her rent, and so the story goes that she made a quilt by candlelight to give to her landlord in lieu of rent. Her quilt is bold in style with stylised flowers in Turkey red, orange and green on a white background. In many ways her style owes more to an American tradition, though the quilting designs are essentially North Country. Phoebe's sister, Phyllis had emigrated to the States and they could well have exchanged patterns.

The period from 1800-1850 has been recorded as the "high point" in traditional English quilting, when both quilting and patchwork were seen at their best.

From 1850 onwards quilting in Britain was certainly influenced by American styles, methods and patterns. An increasing mobility of population meant that people were travelling farther afield and returning with new ideas, which were popularised through the medium of a new vogue in women's craft magazines and books particularly on patchwork and appliqué. Towards the end of the 19th century, the low price of cotton fabrics encouraged the making of both wholecloth and strippy quilts, which could be seamed quickly by machine, prior to being stitched by hand.

Patchwork and appliqué flower quilt (above) made by Phoebe Watson c. 1860-70. (1982-243)

Plain Sewing and Art Work

AS FAR BACK as the mid eighteenth century, there had been many experiments in mechanical sewing; however, the greatest advance came in 1846, when an American, Elias Howe, took out a patent for a lock stitch machine. He was soon followed by Isaac M. Singer from Pittstown, New York, who patented a sewing machine in 1851. It was this machine which proved to be one of the first practical machines to go into general use. Some 10-20 years later, it could easily be purchased in main urban centres of the North of England, such as Newcastle upon Tyne.

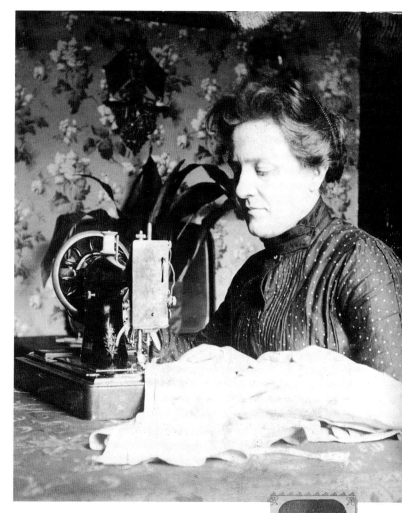

Lady demonstrating her skills at the sewing machine, c.1890, (above) (164,822)

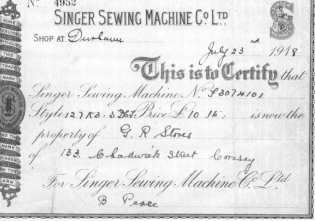

Embroiderers at work. A sewing machine is being used alongside ladies doing hand stitching, 1890 - 1900, (below), (16,308)

Group of ladies at a quilting class in South Shields, Co. Durham, in 1929.
Note the use of the sewing machine, probably being used to piece the quilt top, as well as to stitch the edges.
Most of the work would be completed in hand stitching. (988,648)

The sewing machine was in general use, from the 1870s onwards, and even though most quilting was still done by hand, the machine was invaluable in helping to speed up the preparation of a quilt top. It was particularly useful in the making of strippy and patchwork quilts. In many cases, the machine was also used to complete the quilt with one or two rows of stitches around the outer edge to finish off, creating a much firmer and stronger edge. Many club quilts and sometimes the professionally made quilts were finished in this way, though, in competitions, it was frowned upon, and might even be cause for disqualifying the entrant!

Quilting had always played an important part in the social scene in the country areas of the North Pennine Dales, and it continued to be so. Professional quilters, particularly in the Allendale and Weardale areas, developed a cottage industry which was to influence subsequent quilting styles for the next fifty or so years. People spoke of "stamped" quilts, though these were really quilt tops, which had been carefully designed and marked out with blue pencil. These were then sold to the quilt maker, who would follow the marked pattern with her own stitching.

View of Allendale village, (20,910)

Another form of professional quilting was carried out in the mining villages, from about 1870 onwards. This work was done, more from necessity in hard times, than for any other reason. The miners' wives ran quilt clubs, particularly during the Depression of the 1930s, enabling whole families to be brought up on the proceeds from quilting.

A miner, just home from work with his family. (above left) (12,562)

A miner's family evicted from their house at Silksworth, Co. Durham, in 1891. The makeshift shelter consists of material including quilts. (above right) (5689)

URING THE FIRST thirty years of the twentieth century, there were still many quilters working in the rural and mining areas of the North of England, although the craft had suffered a decline. In 1929, the Rural Industries Bureau had begun to keep records of quilters and had a list of one hundred and seventy, working in County Durham and South Wales, who wanted orders for their work. There were of course many other quilters working for themselves.

Great efforts were made to revive the industry, and in County Durham particularly, Miss Alice Armes, a Durham woman, having been appointed Handicrafts Advisor for the National Federation of Women's Institutes, in the mid 1920s, was influential in stimulating an interest in, and promoting, the home craft of quilting, amongst the Women's Institutes in the County. This soon spread to the neighbouring County of Northumberland, and in 1921 an exhibition of historical quilts was held in Alnwick. Quilting was included in schedules for handicraft exhibitions, the fame of what was then termed 'Durham Quilting' spreading far and wide.

The W.I. magazine **Home and Country**, 1928 Durham supplement for Hamsteels and Quebec, in County Durham, mentions that: -

'In March there was a demonstration of quilting by Mrs. Parker and numerous beautiful articles were shown in this old fashioned craft.' In 1929 Home and Country mentions *'One old man, the husband of a quilt wife, told me proudly that he used to plan out quilt patterns for his mother.'*

NATIONAL FEDERATION OF WOMEN'S INSTITUTES

Introduction to TRADITIONAL ENGLISH QUILTING

LONG ago it was discovered that warmth in bedclothing and garments was much increased if two layers of material were stitched together with a third layer of heat-conserving material between. For this lambs' wool, gathered from the countryside, was found both economical and practical, being light, warm and excellent in the wash. The making of skirts, petticoats, waistcoats and bed covers after this fashion was widely practised in cottage homes less than a hundred years ago. A girl's dowry would include several ' quilts ' or she might make quilted articles for a livelihood. Later the craft nearly died out but it has revived through the unsparing efforts of a few skilled workers and with the aid of the Women's Institute movement and of the Rural Industries Bureau, and beautiful work in the best traditions of British craftsmanship is being done in the North of England and in Wales. This craft demands the highest standard in design and workmanship, and quilters can be justly proud of the way in which this challenge to their skill is being met today.

The early quilters, tired of stitching long straight lines, evolved decorative patterns based on nearby objects—cups, plates, wine glasses provided them with circles; ferns, flowers and leaves with natural forms. These patterns became traditional, increasing in variety and complexity until a quilt became a master-piece of original and beautiful design: they are free and flowing in the North Country (where the traditional shapes include fans, feathers, waves, cords, tassels, and wreaths); in Wales geometrical shapes (circles, triangles and rectangles) are frequently used as frames for spirals, palmettes, Tudor Roses, etc. In the West Country—where unfortunately the craft does not seem to have revived to the same extent—such designs as have survived often show a naturalistic treatment derived from plant forms (e.g. ivy, oak, clover).

The quilt designer, in order that the space to be filled may be ornamented in a decorative and orderly manner without leaving unquilted more than two square inches at most, must choose one or more dominant motifs and set them against a background. Without this principle of main and subordinate theme, the quilt becomes a confused mass of stitchery. First design the central motif, next the corners and borders, then any secondary motifs that the size of the space to be filled may demand, lastly a background contrasting with the main theme, yet harmonious and setting it in the right relief.

It is of the essence of the craft that no two quilted articles should ever be identical in design. True there are traditional motifs but they must always be arranged in accordance with individual taste. Through this union of tradition and novelty, quilting offers a unique opportunity for the ordinary everyday person to create original work which combines utility with artistic merit.

The following outline of quilting technique is intended as a rough guide only; those who wish to practise the craft are strongly advised to take lessons from an expert quilter, for though the actual method may appear comparatively simple, there are many points of detail where skilled and experienced tuition is of the utmost value.

*Ladies from Durham Trefoil Group examining
a patchwork quilt, 3rd February 1960.
(22,414)*

In 1930, the Northumberland Federation held a successful Handicrafts Exhibition at Berwick on Tweed.

'A silver challenge cup for quilting - was won by Mrs.Robson of Allenheads. Thirteen quilts were shown, first class badges being awarded to Wingates, Elsdon, North Sunderland and Seahouses, Amble and Cheswick. Ord, Cheswick and Scremerston received second class badges: machined edges disqualified the rest.'

Also advertised in **Home and Country** were *'Quilt making materials, - Satin, Sateen, Down, Wadding, Kapok etc'* and also *'Quilting - Patterns of traditional designs with leaflets showing method of using. By post 1s 2d – Miss Cooke, Broomhurst, Newton, Chester.'*

Much can be interpreted from the comments made in these magazines. The enthusiasm for quilting was still very much alive as was the competitive spirit of the quilt makers. How interesting to note that quilting patterns were being circulated all around the country at this time.

A prize quilt being shown at Stanley Urban District Council Show on 6th September 1956, (above). (26,836)

ONE OF THE MOST INFLUENTIAL people to revive the craft of quilting was MAVIS FITZRANDOLPH. In 1928, she had been commissioned by the Rural Industries Bureau to carry out an investigation, with the object of discovering some home industry among the women of *'the stricken mining communities'*, during the Depression, which could be developed for a market beyond those areas. Many of the quilters said that, if they could afford to buy good quality materials and received a better rate of payment, they would be able to spend more time on a quilt and produce a better result.

The Bureau helped to subsidise materials, and the first exhibition on commercial lines was held in London at the Little Gallery by Miss Muriel Rose in 1928. It was a great success and stimulated a large number of orders. Classes were organised for the training of experienced quilters.

Largely due to the organisation and enthusiasm of Lady Headlam, wife of the Barnard Castle M.P., the Northern Industries Workrooms were set up in 1933. There were two centres, one in Barnard Castle and the other in Langley Moor, near Durham City.

> *'The Clubs Provide Work For The Unemployed And Offer You Really Beautiful Things'*

Young girls worked, using traditional methods and some of their quilts were commissioned for use in the royal apartments at Windsor. Mrs. Black of West Auckland was most proud of having helped to furnish the Durham Room at the Women's Institute, Denman College in Berkshire.

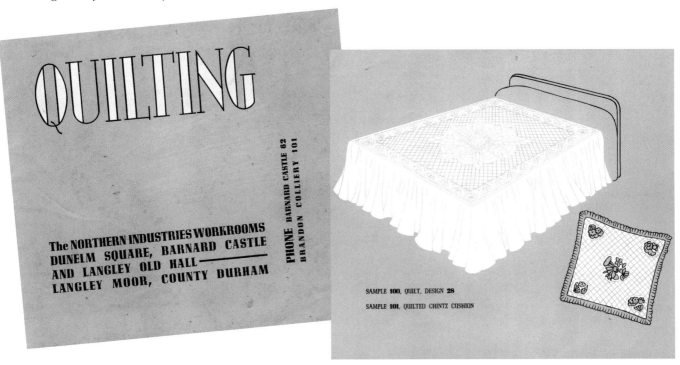

Leaflets publicising the Northern Industries Workshops.

Many of the quilts produced were cot quilts or single bed sized quilts, and they were largely of wholecloth, in silks and satins. Some clothing such as bed jackets, dressing gowns and even toys were also made, and comparatively high prices were charged for these items.

This quilting reached select London retailers, such as Liberty's, as well as private customers. There was a good demand and the work sold well until 1939 when war broke out. The workshops could not continue, with shortage of the quality materials they had been using. There was also a change of direction, with all concentration on the war effort.

During the war years, many of the quilt clubs disbanded. Materials had become scarce, and meanwhile cheap mass-produced bedspreads and eider downs had become popular since the 1920s. The Co-operative Wholesale Society had opened their factory at Pelaw and was producing eiderdowns by the thousand.

PRICE LIST

HAND QUILTING IN VARIOUS DESIGNS		
Silk Quilts	from £8 8 0
Silk on Blanket Quilts	from £7 0 0
Dressing and Evening Jackets	from £4 0 0
Evening and Bed Capes	from £2 10 0
Cushions	from £0 15 0
Car Rugs	from £4 18 6
Foot Muffs	from £1 10 0
Throwovers and Knee-wraps	from £0 19 11
Nightdress and Handkerchief Satchets	from £0 7 6
Darning Pochettes	from £0 7 3
Travelling and Sewing Cases	from £0 4 3

Needle Cases	from £0 1 6
Hot Water Bottle Covers	from £0 10 6
Chintz Workbags	from £0 7 6
Cot Quilts and Pram Covers	from £1 5 0
Babies' Coatees	from £1 5 0
Children's Dressing Gowns	from £1 15 0

MACHINE QUILTING	
Quilts	from £2 10 0
Cot Covers	from £1 1 0
Table Mats	from £0 1 4
Babies' Bibs	from £0 1 6
Shoe Bags	from £0 4 6

BLANKET GOODS	
Gentlemen's Dressing Gowns	from £1 15 0
Ladies' Dressing Gowns, embroidered	from £1 15 0
Hot Water Bottle Covers	from £0 1 11

WOOD WORK	
Bread Boards with carved sheaf	from £0 10 0
Cheese Boards with carved mouse	from £0 6 6
Hand Turned Bowls	from £0 7 6

STUFFED AND WOOLLEN TOYS	
	from 1/-
Elephants, Penguins, Dogs, Mice, Owls, Chicks and Rabbits	

C.W.S. factories at Pelaw on Tyne, c.1911. (94,997)

COOPERATIVE WHOLESALE SOCIETY'S WORK PELAW

A Pelaw eiderdown. (161,682a)

The gradual demise of the older mining communities, and the building of new estates, together with changing social conditions and attitudes had an impact on society in the North East. It became acceptable for women to go out to work. The older generation, however, continued to quilt. Local Education authorities also promoted classes on quilting.

The Pelaw label. (161,682c)

In 1948, Mavis FitzRandolph undertook a scheme to record all that was known of the craft, in the areas of Wales and the North of England. Her survey resulted in a book **Traditional Quilting** in 1954, which contains much of the information we know about the quilts and quilters who were working at that time. Mavis FitzRandolph and Muriel Rose together visited many of the quilters in the North East in April 1952. Their notebook, in the Beamish collections, records names of quilters, details of patterns used and of course all their own comments on both quilts and quilters!

The craft of quilting had nearly died out, but it was revived largely due to the unsparing efforts of a few skilled workers and with the aid of the Women's Institute movement and of the Rural Industries Bureau, under the guidance of Mavis FitzRandolph.

Traditional Quilting book by Mavis FitzRandolph

Much of Mavis's research work in the North Country and Wales has formed the foundation of our knowledge of traditional quilting and was subsequently used by another important figure in the history of quilting. AVERIL COLBY (1900-1983) wrote a number of books on textiles, **Patchwork** in 1958, **Patchwork Quilts** in 1965 and **Quilting** in 1972, though her own particular enthusiasm was for patchwork. Miss Colby was herself a keen quilter, and from 1956-1961, was chairman of the Women's Institute Handicrafts Committee. She did much to promote the craft of quilting, believing strongly in hand stitching as opposed to machined work.

The 1970s was a period of revival for the craft, a National Exhibition of Patchwork being held in London in 1970, organised by the National Federation of Women's Institutes. 350 quilts were exhibited illustrating typical English work.

The older traditional quilters have now gone, but new generations of quilters, inspired by the designs of previous generations, have continued the craft, producing some magnificent work, using the technology of today.

The Quilters' Guild of the British Isles has done much to stimulate interest in the craft and in 1990 launched The British Quilt Heritage Project. The project set out to record '*the special historic character and artistic skills of Britain's quiltmakers and the social and economic conditions in which they worked and also to raise a public awareness and appreciation of this aspect of textile heritage.*' This work was published as **Quilt Treasures** in 1995, and is a remarkable record of the quilts, which survive. As a result of the Guild's work, many quilting groups have been established and the craft is once again flourishing.

Mary Jane Turnbull (above) ran quilting clubs in Winlaton, Co. Durham in the early 1900s. (90,360)

Walter Scott, (above middle) village tailor and quilter of Crookham, Northumberland, c.1900. (27,618)

Mrs. Helen Laidler, quilter of South Shields in the early 1900s. (above right) (19,327)

Maria Armstrong and husband with grandchildren. Maria made quilts at Blackhill, Consett, c.1950, (below) (90,361)

The Page Bank Primitive Methodist Church Sewing Group 1897, (above) (78,229)

Amy Emms, well known traditional quilter, (left).

THE QUILTERS

*Though the older
quilters, who learnt their
craft in the old tradition,
have gone, many of their
quilts still survive, greatly prized
and handed down as family heirlooms.*

URING THE 1800s and early 1900s, most quilts would have been made by quilters, working in their own home, and for their own family. Quilting was very much a family affair, both knowledge of the craft and quilting patterns being handed down from mother to daughter. Many girls learnt at the age of 6-7 years by threading needles for their mothers. Muriel Rose's notebook of 1952, makes mention of Mrs. Isabella Fletcher, who learnt to quilt at Page Bank, Durham, when she was 11 years old, working on quilted stays for the children of the house. She was taught by the 'old lady in the house' in which she was nursemaid.

Some women quilted for a living. The work would be carried out at home and would help to supplement the family income. Usually in this case, communal quilt making was frowned upon, as the highly skilled task of quilting was not regarded as something in which the casual caller could or should participate.

Mrs. Grey of North Shields, in the 1970s, remembered *'My mother was a very keen quilter all her adult life. Eighty years ago she was a dressmaker with two apprentices. During the winter months when trade was slack, the three of them sewed one weekend, made a quilt the next week and I think charged £1.00 for the quilt. Later in the 20s and 30s, when she quilted merely for pleasure, she completed a quilt on her own in her spare time in about 6 weeks, doing them for friends and church bazaars.'*

The tradition of professional quilt marking or "stamping" as it was known, developed in the rural district of Allendale in Northumberland, and Weardale. These professional quilt stampers influenced tremendously the designing of North Country quilts.

Ladies from Rookhope, Weardale, Co. Durham, with their rag mats and quilts, in the 1920s. (above) (19,548)

Collection of printed posters and verse, recording the murder of Joe the Quilter in 1826

East View of the Cottage in Homer's Lane, near Warden, Northumberland, where the Atrocious Murder was committed Tuesday night 3rd Jany 1826. On the body of Joseph Hedley, commonly called 'Joe the Quilter'; a man who had attained to a greater proficiency in quilting than any ever known in the north of England.

JOE the QUILTER.

VERSES, by A. WRIGHT,

DESCRIPTIVE OF THE MANNERS AND HABITS OF

JOSEPH HEDLEY, commonly called Joe the Quilter;

A poor inoffensive Man, aged 80,

Who was found MURDERED in his Cottage near Warden, in the Neighbourhood of Hexham, on Saturday, Jan. 7, 1826. There were not fewer than 44 wounds inflicted in his head, and face, and neck.

—AND the lone cottage on the hill,
Is it without a tenant still?
No. It remained vacant till
'Twas ta'en by Joe the Quilter.

Then it became the main resort,
There lads and lasses went to court,
To chat and have a bit of sport,
With canny Joe the Quilter.

Old Joe hedg'd in a rood of land,
As from the stroke of magic wand
A garden sprung beneath his hand:—
Industrious Joe the Quilter.

His cot secure—his garden neat,
He lov'd the lone and still retreat,
Glad were his neighbours all to meet
With honest Joe the Quilter.

Of each he had some good to say,
Some friendly token to display,
And few could cheer a winter's day,
Like canty Joe the Quilter.

Joe was belov'd by all.—The great
Forgot the lowness of his state,
And at their tables sometimes sate,
Respected Joe the Quilter.

By efforts of superior skill,
He paid these tokens of good-will,
Humble, but independent still,
Was grateful Joe the Quilter.

His quilts with country fame were crown'd,
So neatly stitch'd, and all the ground,
Adorn'd with flowers, or figur'd round;
Oh, clever Joe the Quilter!

Joe's wife was sick, bed-rid, and old,
To ease her pain he spent—he sold,—
Oh, there was never bought for gold,
Such love as Joe the Quilter's.

He was her housewife, doctor, nurse,
But still the poor old soul grew worse,
And she was lifted to her hearse,
By weeping Joe the Quilter.

His labour still supplied their need,
Till eight years' sickness bent the reed,
And then the parish took some heed
Of poor old Joe the Quilter.

And now in widowhood and age,
Frail, fail'd in sight, his hermitage
Was little better than the cage
Of feeble Joe the Quilter.

But there were friends who cheer'd his days,
Money and food they strove to raise,
And—kinder still—reliev'd with praise
The mind of Joe the Quilter.

A favour'd duck was dead, but yet
He had two hens, on which he set
High value, and a cat, the pet
Of tender Joe the Quilter.

These were his wealth; and these to guard,
He'd just receive his work's reward,
And, darkling, homewards trudging hard,
I've met the thoughtful Quilter.

Thus oft from Warden Paper Mill,
He'd toiling climb the weary hill,
Tho' bed and supper, with good will,
Were press'd on Joe the Quilter.

His friends, his hens, his cat, and garden,
He never thought his lot a hard one;
And the old Hermit of High Warden,
They call'd good Joe the Quilter.

Oft in his solitary nook,
With shaking head, but steadfast look,
Through spectacles on godly book,
Was seen the pious Quilter.

His lowly latch was thought secure,
At night he seldom ope'd the door,
Except to lodge the wand'ring poor,—
O! hospitable Quilter.

Who rais'd the tale 'twere vain to scan,
But far and wide the story ran,
That there was scarce a wealthier man
Than poor old Joe the Quilter.

Satan, by this vain tale, 'tis said,
Had put it in some monster's head,
To violate the lowly shed,
And MURDER Joe the Quilter.

Miss'd by his friends at Walwick Grange,
Who thought his few days absence strange,
They sought the cot—and—awful change!
There lay the murder'd Quilter.

We pass the horrid scene of blood,
For when hath feeling heart withstood
The grief of the afflicted good?—
All mourn'd for Joe the Quilter.

Joe kill'd!—What Joe, whom all revere!
The sceptic, with sardonic sneer,
Cries, 'Virtue is rewarded here!
Witness good Joe the Quilter.'

Pause infidel—think Sovereign love
Will thus its martyr'd servants prove,
To fit them for their crowns above;
So be it with Joe the Quilter.

Know then, ye proud ones of the earth,
How light weigh greatness, wealth, and birth,
To lowly Virtue's heavenly worth,
And envy Joe the Quilter.

Newcastle: Marshall, Printer.

Whitehall, January 17th, 1826.

WHEREAS

IT hath been humbly represented unto the King, that on the Evening of Tuesday the 3rd instant

JOSEPH HEDLEY,

Residing alone in a Cottage in Homer's Lane, near Warden, in the County of Northumberland, Quilter, was Inhumanly MURDERED, by some Person or Persons unknown.

His Majesty, for the better Apprehending and bringing to Justice the Person or Persons concerned in the Atrocious Murder above mentioned, is hereby pleased to promise his most gracious PARDON to any one of them, (except the Person who actually Committed the same) who shall discover his Accomplice or Accomplices therein, so that he, she, or they, may be Apprehended and Convicted thereof.

ROBERT PEEL.

And, as further encouragement a REWARD of

One Hundred Guineas

Is hereby offered by the Overseers of the Poor of the Parish of Warden aforesaid, to any Person (except as aforesaid) who shall discover the said Offender or Offenders, so that he, she, or they, may be Apprehended and Convicted of the said Offence.

E. DICKENSON, PRINTER, HEXHAM.

Joe the Quilter

Hedley

Joe the Quilter's Cottage

JOSEPH HEDLEY, better known as *"Joe the Quilter"*, was born sometime between 1745 and 1750. Numerous accounts have been written about his life and occupation as a quilter, but he has been remembered mostly for his horrendous murder in 1826. The Newcastle Chronicle recorded a full account of this unsolved mystery and verses were written describing his life and sad demise. Posters offered One Hundred Guineas Reward *'to any person who shall discover the said offender'*. **The Monthly Chronicle of North Country Lore and Legend** gave a vivid description, much later in 1887, of the happenings of that night.

Joe had, in his younger days, been apprenticed to a tailor, though realising that cutting coats and trousers was not his particular forté, he had developed a skill, which led him to adopt the profession of quilting. Joe showed exquisite taste in devising intricate designs delineating flowers, fruit and figures. First he cut out the patterns in cardboard, then laid them on the cloth, and with a chalk or pencil, outlined the flower or leaf which his customer had selected. He became popular with the '*lady members of families*', and his services appear to have been greatly sought after. His work was sent as far afield as Ireland and America, and his fame was renowned.

Joe spent the latter days of his life alone in a small thatched cottage in Homer's Lonnen, in the parish of Warden, near Hexham, overlooking the river Tyne. The cottage was quite lonely and Joe became known as "*The Hermit of Warden*". The quilter had been married, however, though his married life had turned out to be more of a burden and a severe drain on his slender resources. His wife had been much older than him and had been bed ridden for eight years before her death and Joe had had to look after her.

*Engraving of Joe the quilter's cottage,
from a drawing by R. Donkin of Warden,
published by Davison of Alnwick in 1826. (30,802)*

East View of the Cottage in Homer's Lane, near Warden, Northumberland, where the Atrocious Murder was committed Tuesday night 3rd Jany 1826. On the body of Joseph Hedley, (commonly called "Joe the Quilter") a man who had attained to a greater proficiency in quilting than any ever known in the north of England.

Published by W. Davison Alnwick.
Drawn by R. Donkin, Warden Jany 10, 1826.

In his spare time, Joe had reclaimed a piece of wasteland, which he cultivated and grew fruit. He was known for entertaining pedlars and itinerants, who brought him news of happenings up and down the country. It is even said that he enjoyed conniving at smuggling! One evening on Tuesday, January 3rd 1826, he returned to his cottage, having been at Walwick Grange in the afternoon. That same evening William Herdman, a labourer from Wall village called to see him, staying a few minutes. Joe had a good fire and was preparing his supper. Later in the evening, a female pedlar, who had lost her way, called and enquired the way to Fourstones. She was the last person to see Joe alive.

By Saturday, the neighbours had become alarmed and the cottage door was burst open. Joe was found savagely murdered. All efforts to discover the murderer were fruitless. The only possible motive for the crime was considered to have been the hope of securing a fortune that Joe was supposed to have accumulated from his quilting. Joe's cottage was pulled down in 1872, so that all landmarks of the tragedy have gone.

Very few of Joe's quilts survive, though the ones that do, exhibit some very fine quilting. A favourite design became known as *Old Joe's Chain*.

TO BE SOLD
BY AUCTION,
JAMES ROBSON, AUCTIONEER.
On Wednesday the 29th March 1826,
At HOMER'S HOUSE, in the Parish of Warden,
Northumberland,
ALL THE
HOUSEHOLD
FURNITURE,
Belonging the Late Unfortunate Joseph Hedley,
COMMONLY CALLED
JOE THE QUILTER;
CONSISTING of a Dresser and Shelves, 1 Clock, 1 Bed,
1 Press, 1 Kitchen Table, 1 Corner Cupboard, &c.
The Sale to commence precisely at one o'Clock.

Barker, Printer, Hexham.

In the early 1800s, commemorative textile prints
were often used as centrepieces for quilts, and for
patchwork. These panels sometimes record a
particular event in a commemorative medallion, or
depict an ornamental flower basket or wreath. They
were printed on cotton and were used between 1797
and 1835. Joe used one such panel in a quilt owned
by a Mrs. Gibson of Hexham. A very similar quilt
with printed panel centrepiece, from the Haydon
Bridge area, made c. 1820-25, may also be Joe's
work, though the border pillar print fabric was
probably added at a slightly later date. Joe's
customers would have supplied him with materials
from which he pieced their quilts. The quilt
illustrates some fine stitching. (1972-658.120)

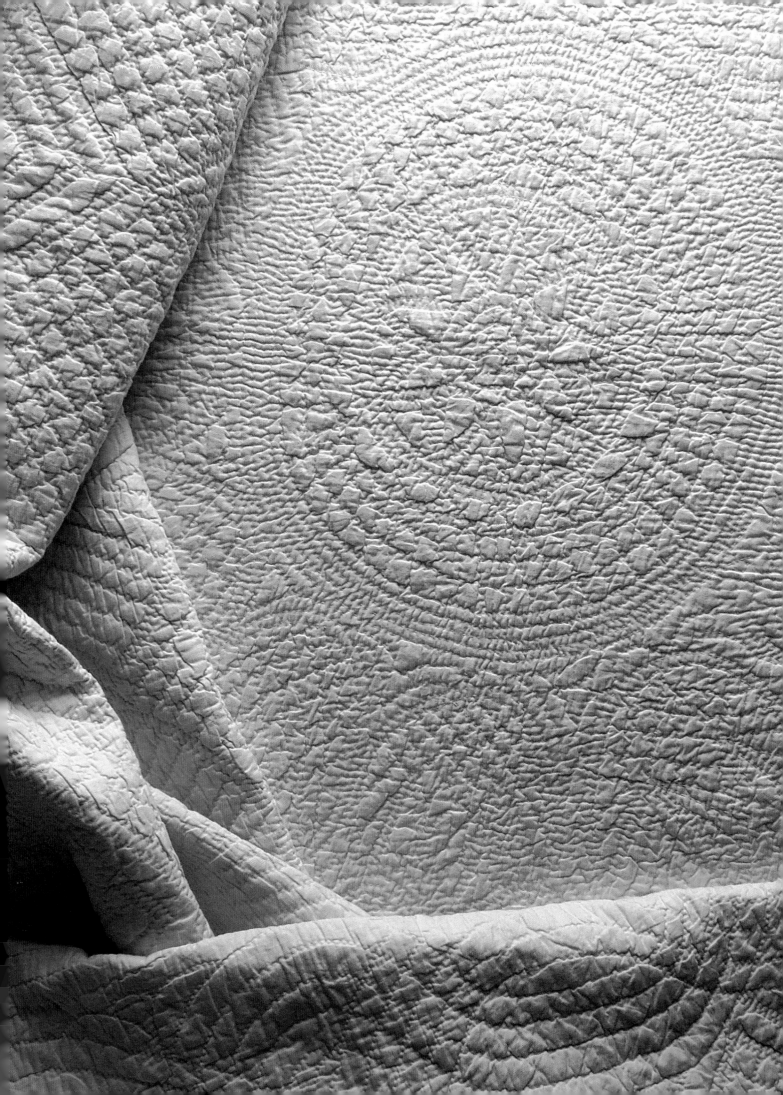

One of the last quilts to have been made by Joe was bought directly from him in 1820, by the English family who owned Humshaugh Mill, only a short distance away from where Joe himself lived. It is interesting that this quilt was passed down in the English family to James Armstrong Herdman of Wall village, of whom the William Herdman of our story was probably an ancestor. This wholecloth quilt illustrates the *trail, worm* and *fan,* typical of his work. (1979-442)

George

Gardiner

George Gardiner

REGRETFULLY VERY LITTLE IS KNOWN about GEORGE GARDINER other than that he kept the village shop at Smelt Mill Cottages, Dirt Pot, Allenheads in Northumberland, in about the 1880s. Born probably around 1853, and brought up by his grandmother, he became a draper, running a drapery and millinery business with his wife Sarah, who was a milliner from along the dale.

The North Pennine Dales of Weardale and Allendale were important centres for the lead mining industry in Britain, and Allenheads mine in particular was the largest single mine in the northern ore field producing approximately 260,000tons of lead between 1729 and 1896. A remote area, the communities within these dales were amongst the highest and most isolated settlements in the country. Lead mining, the main occupation, was practised alongside farming and quarrying, many of the lead miners participating in dual occupations.

Wholecloth quilt in the distinctive Allenheads style, which George Gardiner developed. (1963-58) (above) (30,618)

View of Allenheads, from School Hill, c.1900. (9312)

Unusually for the time, George Gardiner was not employed in the lead mining industry, though his trade as a draper did depend to quite an extent on the prosperity of the industry. By the end of the 19th century, the industry had collapsed, the price of lead having dropped from £21 per ton in the 1850s to £9.50 per ton in the 1890s. The industry and local society suffered a deathblow.

Many families emigrated to America for work or moved away into the coalmines. George meanwhile made a name for himself by trimming hats and girls would walk from Allendale or over the fells from Wearhead to get their hats trimmed by him. He developed a further reputation for marking the patterns onto quilt tops and became well known as a professional "stamper". Subsequently Allenheads and the Allendale area became noted as a quilt design and stamping centre. Although known as stamped quilts, the designs were actually drawn onto the material with a blue pencil. To this day these quilts can be easily recognised by their blue pencil markings. Quilts were marked out and sent all round the country.

Detail of lover's knot pattern on a stamped wholecloth quilt, pre 1906. (2001-41.1)

Detail of an Allenheads quilt, illustrating a typical corner design
with Prince of Wales' Feathers. (1991-127)

George Gardiner brought about a revolution in quilt design, introducing an entirely new style to quilting which became popular in Weardale and throughout Northumberland. Typical quilts consisted of an elaborate central floral design with *roses* and *feathers* and an outer border often of *hammock* or *fleur de lis*, linking elaborate corner designs, with an overall *diamond* infill for the background. He taught his wife's two nieces to quilt and mark patterns, however his best-known pupil was Elizabeth Sanderson.

One of Elizabeth Sanderson's most popular quilt designs has become known as the "Sanderson Star". This quilt was used by Elizabeth Allison (nee Richardson), who was born in 1849 and lived at Ouston in Co. Durham. It is a fine example in blue and white cotton with a reverse in white cotton sateen, which was probably made c.1890. (1985-148)

Elizabeth Sanderson

The Sanderson Star

ELIZABETH SANDERSON was born in 1861 and lived at Fawside Green Farm in Allenheads. She did little or no farming herself, leaving the farm management to her sister. Having been apprenticed to George Gardiner, Elizabeth built up an even greater reputation as quilter, quilt designer, and quilt "stamper". A number of her quilts still survive bearing the distinctive blue pencil markings of the pattern. Miss Sanderson charged between 1/ 6d and 2/- for marking a quilt top up until the 1930s, and she could mark two quilts a day.

The quilt tops were ordered by farmers' wives when they required something a little special or for a grand occasion such as a wedding. The Misses Johnson of Dotland Farm, in Hexhamshire remembered the packman travelling goods, including several quilt tops, from farm to farm, reaching some of the most remote areas. Several fine examples of these quilts were seen at Dotland, and were much prized by the family. The quilt tops were also sold from the local Co-op store.

A pink and white cotton baskets quilt, pieced and "stamped" by Elizabeth Sanderson, is the only known example of this pattern, to have been pieced and designed by her.

The quilt was sewn by Mrs. DEBORAH ADAMSON of Rookhope in 1912. The outer border illustrates the *Weardale chain* pattern, which was used on a number of her quilts. (1963-56)

Fawside Green Farm, Allenheads

Sanderson Star quilt in pink and white cotton, quilted in twist, rose, leaf with diamond infill. The quilt came from Haydon Bridge, Northumberland. (1972-658.117)

Elizabeth became so adept and well known for her "stamping" that she employed other women from the Allendale area, taking them on as apprentices to learn the trade of quilt marking. Her first apprentice was Mrs. Coulthard, the daughter of a farming butcher, from Wearhead, who left school at the age of 14 in the 1890s, and walked the six miles over the fells to Allenheads, taking with her, provisions for a week. She worked for a full year without pay, and at the end of that time, became a paid hand, earning 4/- a week with her board and lodging. She could mark two quilts a day and would charge 1/9d each. She also used to mark quilts for the Newcastle Co-op.

At the age of 77 years in 1962, when still marking quilts, Mrs. Peart of Allendale recalled the days of her training as Elizabeth's second apprentice. She served for six months without pay at the age of 14, providing her own food. She worked from 8.00am until 7.00pm with an hour off for lunch and half an hour for tea. She served for six years being paid 2/- per week in the second year and then up to 4/-. By 1952 she was charging 5/- to mark a quilt top on cotton sateen or 7/- if on silk. Her daughter remembered being *'sick of*

the sight of them' as a child *'and they would all be to carry to the post'.*

Mrs. Mallaby, born and brought up in Allenheads, was the third apprentice. Her mother and grandmother had both been quilters, doing work for the chapel, and as a child Mrs. Mallaby would thread needles for the sewing meetings. She was apprenticed for the first six months without pay, but afterwards worked for 5/- per week. She could remember people sending their quilt tops by post to Allenheads to be marked. Seven or eight would arrive at a time. The centre would be marked on a large round table and the borders on an oblong one.

Elizabeth designed and marked quilts with her apprentices, until she died in 1933 at the age of 72. She has left quite a legacy and in particular, one of her most distinctive designs, that of the Sanderson Star has been passed down through the Allendale school of "stampers", many of these quilts surviving

today, in varying contrasting colourways, such as Turkey red and white, pink and white, and blue and white. The quilts consist of a framed eight pointed star surrounded by alternating coloured borders.

Mrs. Peart of Juniper Farm, Allendale had her own apprentices, one of them being Miss Mary Fairless. Mary was born in 1908 at Park Gill, Allendale and lived there until she was 25 years old, when she moved to Hay Leazes, and then spent eleven years working with Mrs. Peart. Mary's younger sister also helped on the farm at Juniper.

Mary spent her time marking quilt tops, though not doing any stitching.

This quilt was the first that she completed as part of her apprenticeship at 21 years of age in 1929. The material was called Zephyr and was purchased from Allendale Co-op. (1993-212)

Miss Mary Fairless with Mrs. Jennie Peart in 1935 at Juniper Farm.
Both were well known quilters.

The influence of the Allendale school of markers cannot be under estimated in quilt making in the North East in the following years. Allendale quilts are normally easy to identify if only for the fine quality of their marking. The quilts and their designs were often copied. The Sanderson Star design certainly influenced this quilt, which was made by Mrs. Lumsden as a wedding present for her grand daughter, Mary Ann Bethwaite of Craghead in 1916. The star has been converted to a four-leaf clover. Perhaps this was an Irish family using a lucky symbol.

The quilt of green and pink cotton sateen repeats the alternating borders of the Sanderson design, quilted in very similar style in *twist, plait* and *running feather.* (1981-303)

IN THE POST WAR YEARS, from the 1950s onwards, quilting suffered a serious decline. Quilts were regarded as being old fashioned and indeed there were few women who knew how to quilt, having lost the habit of passing the knowledge down from one generation to the next. A changing lifestyle meant that more women went out to work and had no time for the luxury or the wish to quilt.

By the 1960s, only a small group of the older traditional quilters were still at work and mostly these were people who had learnt the craft from their mothers. Mary Lough and Florence Fletcher were two such ladies.

MARY LOUGH, born in 1886, had come to quilting somewhat late in life, though she was certainly from a family of quilters, with her mother, grandmother and aunts all proficient in the craft. She had learnt to quilt threading needles by candlelight, for her mother who had come from the West Allen area. Her grandmother had been a dressmaker from Alston and some of her quilts, made in about 1860, were still treasured by the family.

Mary Lough & Florence Fletcher

Mary Lough at her quilting frame. The photo was taken, when she was 81 years old, a year before she died in 1968. (10,659)

Detail (left) from quilt made by Mary Lough (1989-217)

Mary Lough finishing off an eiderdown (top left) (29,330)
Mary Lough wearing one of her quilted jackets. (top centre) (43,178)
Mary Lough driving a horse drawn hay rake, probably 1930-40. (top right) (43,526)
Mary Lough draws a design onto greaseproof paper, and then pricks it through onto the material. (centre right) (29,329)

Mary found time to help run the family farm, at Chapman Hill, Witton le Wear, as well as undertaking embroidery, quilting, not to mention cooking! Not only did she design, quilt and sew, she found her own supply of feathers from the farm's geese! She produced some wonderfully fine work on pure silk, using flowing *rose, feather* and *goosewing* patterns, most of these being produced in her later years. It is likely that Mary devised the method of making a border pattern, such as the *running feather*, turn a corner in an elegant fashion. Mary also found time to work for Dewhirst's, advertising their Sylko threads, and had an invoice returned for not charging enough for her work!

The wedding, probably at Tow Law, of Mary Teasdale and William Lough, a railway worker. Mary's father, Charles Brunton Teasdale, standing to the right of the bride, bought Chapman Hill Farm in 1930. He was mine manager at West Thornley Colliery. (43,173)

Her daughter recalled that *'she travelled all over the British Isles teaching, and articles quilted by her were sent to Australia and America - she made quilts, bed jackets, cushion covers and a housecoat which has been exhibited in the Victoria and Albert Museum'*. Mary Lough was one of the first North Country quilters to teach quilting and ran courses throughout the country.

Detail of a wholecloth quilt made by Mary Lough, c. 1950-1960. The quilt has been made in crepe de chine and the quilting pattern consists of a central feather circle, surrounded by scissor pattern and with a border of feather wreaths and diamond infill. (1989-217)

In the early 1950s, there was no formal City and Guilds' Diploma for quilting, even though various Education Authorities had run evening classes. Mary Lough taught classes for quilting and Florence Fletcher attended her classes becoming a skilled quilter and going on to teach City and Guilds Diploma all round the British Isles.

FLORENCE FLETCHER was born in the early 1900s, and lived in Weardale most of her life. She worked with the Rural Industries Bureau and actively helped to rescue a number of old quilts, which would be preserved in the museums of the region.

In 1955, Florence Fletcher and Mavis FitzRandolph collaborated on the production of a booklet **QUILTING, Traditional Methods and Design**, published by Dryad Press.

This was one of the first books to describe the design and pattern planning methods for traditional quilt making.

'The way in which teachers instruct their classes is of the greatest importance to the future of the craft because, on this the survival of the tradition depends. When holding a quilting class in any district, an enterprising teacher, will ask students to try to find old quilts and bring them to the class, where the history of the quilt, its age and place of origin should be discovered as far as possible, and the quilted patterns examined and discussed. It may be a patchwork bedcover whose quilted pattern has hardly been noticed by the owner; it may be a beautiful and treasured piece of work or rather roughly quilted; but something of interest can be found in the pattern'.

The book ran to five editions and did a lot to promote the craft to those who had not learnt from the older generations.

Florence Fletcher, was also instrumental in assisting Mavis FitzRandolph, when she visited Weardale and Teesdale and was able to help with introductions to some of the quilters still working in both Dales. A fine quilt, designed and made by Florence Fletcher in 1958, illustrates the use of the more modern fabric, cotton poplin and the design of *pineapples* and *wheat sheaves* is very much her own.

Quilt in cotton poplin, made by Florence Fletcher in 1958. (1963-59)

Detail of pineapple on reverse of above quilt, (left).

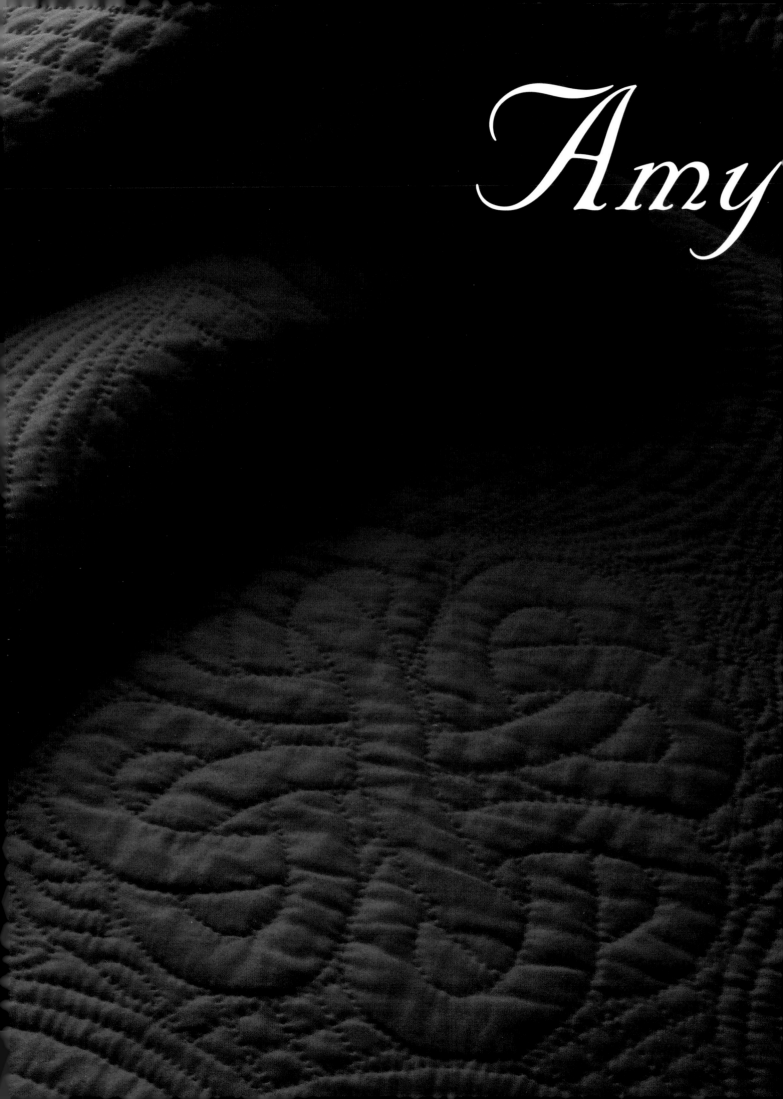

Amy

Emms

Amy Emms quilting in her cottage at
Huntshieldford, Daddry Shield,
Weardale, in the 1970s.

AMY EMMS was born in the village of Fulwell, near Sunderland, on the North East coast in 1904. Her father had died before she was born, so Amy was brought up by a mother who worked all hours to make ends meet. Besides going out to work, her mother quilted in order to provide additional income for the family. *'She was a real country woman, carrying on the tradition of quilting which had been in her family for generations.'* Amy learnt to thread needles and by the age of 14 was quilting alongside her mother, who also ran a quilting club.

Leaving school at 14, Amy went to a private Shorthand Academy, where she learnt business training and went to work in an office. In 1920, she met Albert Emms, who worked for Hartley Woods, the stained glass manufacturers, and they married in 1924. Married life started in the family home and Amy continued to quilt with her mother, bringing up a young family at the same time.

Amy joined the British Legion, where she became a Standard Bearer. It wasn't long before her skills as a quilter were discovered and a full size quilt was made to assist their fundraising. Amy continued to run evening classes for the British Legion and to undertake her own commissions, making beautiful quilts for Lady Havelock-Allan.

*Quilt made for the author by
Amy Emms in the 1970s.*

*Amy Emms with her British Legion quilting class
in Sunderland in 1944. (4050)*

In 1951, when her children had left school, she was encouraged by the Education Authority to take evening classes, and between 1953 and 1954, worked with Mary Lough, in order to satisfy the Authority that she had the knowledge and skills to continue teaching. A letter was sent to Mary Lough 'with much appreciation of your help and advice', signed by a number of pupils including Amy.

Amy's pride and joy was the wedding dress she made for her daughter, Olive's wedding in 1957, and she regarded it as her greatest achievement. Two years later, Amy and Albert bought a cottage at Daddry Shield in Weardale, ready for Albert's retirement in 1967. Sadly, after a very short retirement, he died suddenly in 1971.

Amy would not let this become the end of her life, and quilting became the focus, providing her with good company, entertainment and so much more. In 1970, Beamish, The North of England Open Air Museum, had just been started, and the author, Rosemary Allan, had been appointed to the post of Assistant Keeper of Social History, as the first member of staff. Rosemary had known Amy previously and appreciating her special skills as a quilter, asked Amy if she would like to come and demonstrate quilting at a Crafts Weekend being held at the museum. Amy never looked back, taking on a new lease of life.

'That was a lovely day and I sat and talked, with my 'bits and pieces' in front of me and my frame and equipment, answering all the questions folks asked. The room was very old fashioned and the building a piece of history. One little lad of about four stood in front of me and studied me very carefully before asking, 'Do you live here missus?' 'No, sonny, not here' I replied but everyone had a good laugh as he obviously thought that the elderly lady sitting there with her quilting was a permanent part of the fittings!'

Amy's visits to Beamish opened up new horizons and her quilting career took off. Her gentle, patient and humorous, no-nonsense personality, let alone her wonderful skills as a quilter, meant that she was much in demand, at quilt shows and exhibitions. She corresponded regularly in the Quilters' Guild magazine and became a celebrity, being awarded the M.B.E. in 1984, for *'services to quilting'*. At the age of 86 years, she wrote her book ***Amy Emms' Story of Durham Quilting***.

Amy was probably the last of a long line of traditional quilters who had learnt the craft from the older generation. She had her own pupils in classes, which she taught at Westgate in Weardale. Elsie Walton, one of those pupils, ran the 240-acre Old Park Farm, at Westgate, Weardale, with her husband, but Elsie still found time to quilt. Here the author is seen observing Amy at one of those classes in 1978.

Amy never stopped quilting. At the age of 94, she was still travelling around the country attending quilt shows. Her life had witnessed a change from traditional quilting as a country craft to quilting as an art form. Amy died on June 17th 1998.

Patchwork quilt in wool, (right)
made c. 1910 (1973-517)

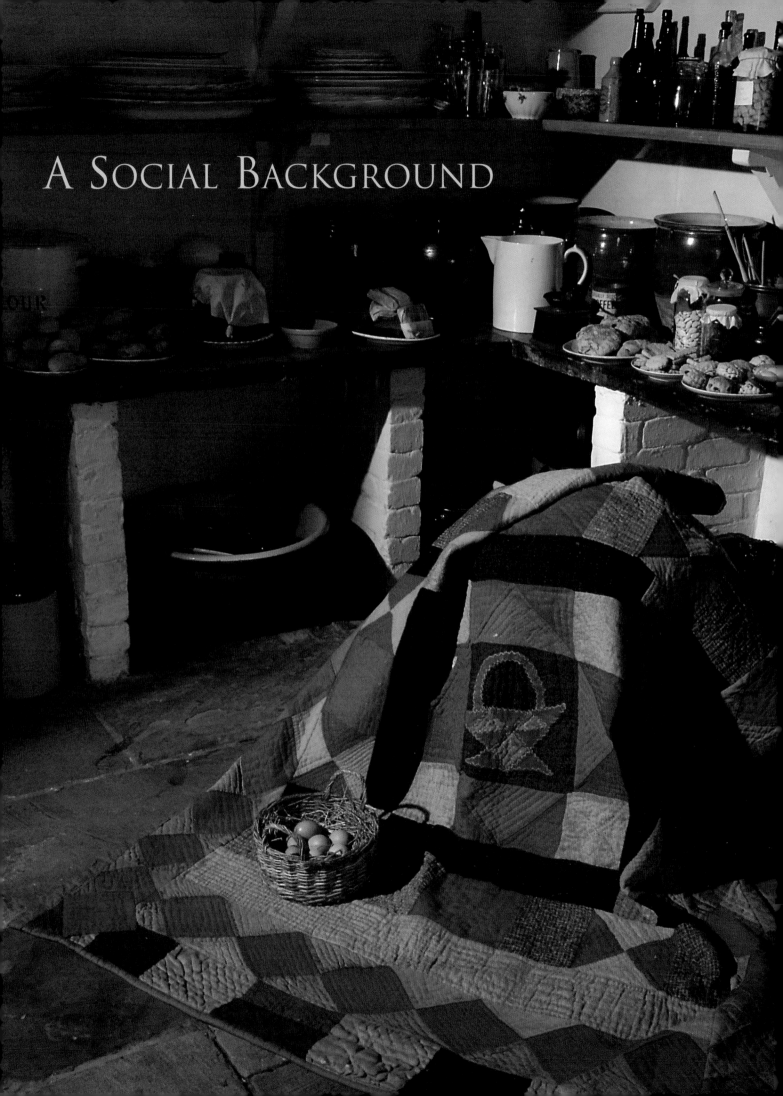

A SOCIAL BACKGROUND

The Rural Quilters

'When a woman had patched a bed quilt, she invited her neighbours to help quilt it, for which purpose it was stretched with its lining on a long frame and sewn across. Sometimes they drew figures with saucers, oyster shells, etc. In later times tea and cakes were given; formerly a cold posset consisting of new milk, sugar, currants and rum (or beer). When they could get it, the milk was taken warm from the cow and milked fast into the 'piggin' so as to froth it'.

SO ALFRED EASTHER wrote in his glossary of the Dialect of Almondbury and Huddersfield in 1883. In rural areas, at one time, every house would have had several quilts, and in earlier days every farmhouse would have had a set of quilting frames. Quilting was often a recognised part of the farm routine, in areas where farming and lead mining were dual occupations. The husband would work in the lead mines during the week, living in the mine "shop", only returning home at weekends. The wife was left to run the farm or smallholding.

Rosalie Bosanquet edited some wonderful memories of old Northumberland, collected by the Cambo Women's Institute, In **The Troublesome Times**, in 1929. *'Closed beds, box beds, or cupboard beds were common, until twenty or thirty years ago in Northumberland. Forty years ago, almost every hind's kitchen had two box beds. On the beds were fine patchwork quilts, or beautiful quilts, quilted with long flowing patterns, such as are still made at home.'*

In about 1911, MISS HUMBLE of Wearhead, marked and quilted for a living, and was never in bed after 5.00am in the morning. The farmwork was done by 9.00am and then she quilted until mid-day. After dinner, she would feed the calves and finish any other jobs that had to be done, before returning to her quilting. She never quilted by lamplight.

Sweeping hay at St.John's Chapel, Weardale, c.1910. (3501)

Quilting was sometimes allied to dressmaking and tailoring. Mrs. Edward Pearson of Cambo in Northumberland, (who died in 1927 at the age of 82) recalled *'My father's aunt was a dressmaker and used to go out to the farmhouses for a month at a time, dressmaking, quilting and patchin'* .

John Lee tells the story of that well-known Weardale quilter HANNAH EMMERSON *(right)* :

'Her husband, a miner and small farmer, died of the miner's dread disease in his early fifties, the farm was mortgaged and her husband, in his last days, asked her not to sell it. She made her promise to him and alone carried out all the work that was normally done by a man on the farm. On top of that she charred, made beautiful quilts by the dim light of candles, brought new lives into the world in a wide area and did the necessary duties when life expired. She was never in debt and in tiny sums, shown by receipts, wiped off the mortgage, dying at the age of eighty-two with the unchanged name of Hannah Emmerson of high-lying windswept Wham'.

POLLY RHODES of Hunwick, Co. Durham, born in 1856, started to sew this fine patchwork and appliqué quilt in pink, yellow and green cotton, when she was nine years old. She completed it some five years later, in 1870. The quilt was made for a four-poster bed and is a good example of an elaborate patchwork design, showing signs of American influence. The quilt was inherited by Polly's niece, Mrs Weighill, seen here with the quilt.

A view of Weardale, Co. Durham.

ISABELLA WILES, born at Wears Bank, Wolsingham, in Weardale, in 1914, had also worked with Mary Lough and used many of her patterns, such as *feather, twist, rose* and *goosewing*. She produced some magnificent work in cotton poplin as well as pure silk. She made a special presentation quilt to be given, by the tenants of the Lumley Estate to the Earl of Scarbrough.

Group of ladies at Rookhope, Weardale, with their quilts and mats. (19,548)
Isabella Wiles of Wolsingham, at the quilting frame.

The Quilting Clubs

Quilting Clubs probably originated in the mining villages of Northumberland and Durham, during the latter half of the 19th century. The region's wealth and economy depended upon its mineral resources, in particular that of coal. In the Great Northern Coalfield, the coal owners provided the miners and their families with houses and a supply of coal, free in exchange for labour. However, if the miner or main wage earner could not work, the family might be evicted from their home. Accidents in the pit were common and there was little in the way of compensation.

QUILTING BECAME AN IMPORTANT MEANS OF SURVIVAL in many pit communities, providing a lifeline and a means of supporting the quilter and her family. Mining families, in these close-knit communities always depended upon each other in times of adversity. There are a number of records of pit wives, who brought up their families on the proceeds from quilting, when their husbands had either been injured or killed.

The first clubs began in about 1870, but flourished particularly during the strikes and depressions of the 1920s and 1930s, when all too often, a miner's wife became a widow, or her husband had become disabled, and unable to work.

Back to back miners' houses at Twizell, Co. Durham, in the 1920s. (below) (20,262)

Typical scene in a pit cottage, of child cosily wrapped up in a wholecloth quilt. (above) (168,177)

Wholecloth quilt. (left) quilted in strips of running feather c. 1920-30 (2004-141)

The clubs operated a hire purchase system, the work being done at home. The quilter needed to find some twenty or so clients willing to buy quilts, and they would pay the quilter weekly or fortnightly until they had covered the full cost of the quilt. This enabled the quilter to buy all her materials and to produce one quilt every 2-3 weeks. It also enabled the purchaser time to save enough money to pay for the quilt. Everyone paid about 1/- per week until £3.10s was collected. When the first quilt had been completed, the members would draw out of a hat to see who would get the first quilt. The cost of making a quilt was approximately £2.5s so the quilter made a profit of about £1 in the 1920s. The price of a quilt would have been about the same as a miner's wage for a fortnight. A quilter's "wage" was therefore very hard earned.

Mavis FitzRandolph recorded a number of quilters who had run quilting clubs: *'Mrs. Hope said that her mother, in 1887, was left a widow with five children and 'brought them up by quilting'; when the four daughters were old enough they helped her at the frame; four working together could turn out four quilts weekly.'*

Usually, however, a woman would work on her own ensuring that the stitching was consistent. For the most part, the stitching on club quilts was not as fine as on other quilts. Time meant money and the faster the quilt was made the sooner the quilter got paid. The clubs became extremely popular; one woman recorded forty members in her club.

Photograph of the interior of a miner's house at Marley Hill, Co. Durham, part of a report by Dr.Darra Mair, on the Sanitary Conditions of miners' housing in 1907. Note the strippy quilt on the bed. (15,872)

These quilts tended to be of wholecloth, that is of plain material on one or both sides, concentrating the design within the stitching. Sometimes a border of a contrasting printed material would be added to provide interest. The stitching was often a large central pattern with outer border and *diamond infill*. Strippy quilts were also popular in the quilt clubs, and were made for everyday use. They could be produced from left over strips from other quilts, and as the pattern could be marked on, in the frame, they were less complicated to make.

Mrs. SALLY RANSON of New Seaham, County Durham, was born in 1870. When she became a miner's widow, she managed to raise a family of four by making quilts and running a quilt club in the 1890s. She died in 1956 at the age of eighty-six. The printed border on this quilt has been carefully mitred at the corners, and the quilting is in strips of *running feather* set on a central circle enclosing eight *roses*. An outer border of *twist* on the printed fabric completes the quilt. (1971-306)

Mrs. STEWART of Bowburn, Durham was also a widow making her living from quilting and running quilt clubs. 1/- per week for twenty weeks was paid for this quilt, which was never used. This quilt is reversible, one side being made from cream sateen with a blue and cream printed border, whilst the other side in pink sateen has a printed border in pink and cream. The quilted centre is composed of a *feather circle* enclosing *flowers* and *leaves*. In the corners are stylised *leaves*, linked by an inner border of *hammock* on a *diamond* infill background. The design is imaginative and very much Mrs. Stewart's own.

(1971-374)

Reverse of Mrs. Stewart's quilt, illustrating quilting patterns below.

Mrs. M. E. SHEPHERD of Amble, Northumberland, ran many quilt clubs, and her daughter recalls; - *'I had to go out and knock on peoples' doors and ask them if they wanted to join our club.'* She also found time to make quilts for her own family, and produced a fine one for her son in anticipation of his marriage, however he remained a bachelor, and the quilt was never used. Mrs. Shepherd's mother had been brought up on Coquet Island, off the North East coast, and had received little education. Her grandmother had died when the seventh child was born.

'My mother and her sister then did all the sewing and knitting for the family; under clothing, shirts, dresses, mats, socks, fancy work and quilts. They sewed for what was then called the bottom drawer, which was their preparation for marriage. They both married miners. Their married life began with a strike, so they quilted. Wages were small so they went on quilting to help out. Then my father was injured, later deprived of compensation so my mother went on quilting. She had quilting clubs taking on twenty at a time, completing one every fortnight. The patterns were drawn first on brown paper then cut out for use. She drew the pattern on the material in a day and a half, improving on them over the years.'

The border design has been made up of a more unusual *shell* pattern, perhaps being influenced by her Coquet Island background. However, when asked about the corner design she said *'Oh that was taken from the seat of a bentwood chair!'*. (1980-744)

Wartime rationing of textile materials hastened the demise of the quilt clubs. Fabrics were in short supply; the fashion for wholecloth quilts was declining and most people had other priorities than quilting.

Chapel and Signature Quilts

During the 19th century, there was a huge and rapid expansion of the coal mining industry in the Great Northern Coalfield, requiring an expanded work force. People came, not only from the Northumbrian countryside, but also from Cumberland, Scotland, Ireland, Yorkshire and Cornwall. They brought with them their own dialects, customs and traditions and were integrated into the local population.

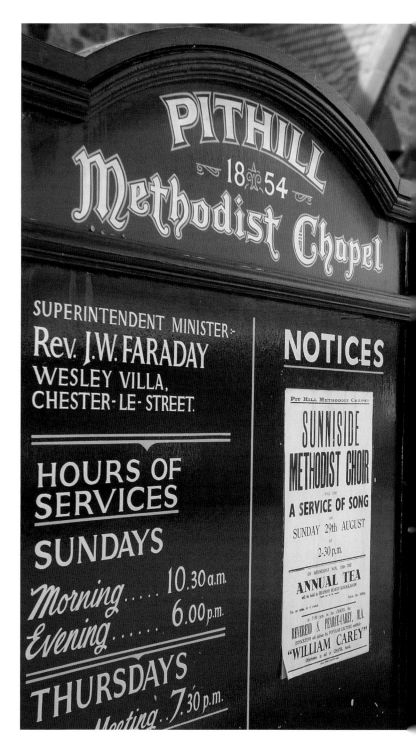

AS THESE MINING COMMUNITIES developed and flourished, so did the churches and Methodist chapels, fulfilling distinct social and spiritual needs of their members. Sunday schools, Men's Bible classes, Temperance groups and the Ladies' Sewing Circles thrived. Many of the Chapel quilts were made from Turkey red and white material with appropriately contrasting embroidery.

Unfinished coverlet consisting of panels of printed texts, machine stitched together. (1992-76)

Illustration from The British Workman, showing a patient reading texts on this patchwork quilt. (15,772)

Most of these quilts do tend to date from the mid 19th century onwards. **Hobbies** magazine in 1899 mentions, *'It is said that invalids find considerable pleasure in such coverlets, but it is necessary to consult individual taste in the selection of the mottos. Others find comfort in texts or lines from favourite hymns. The words are sometimes arranged upon the coverlets that the occupants of neighbouring beds can read inscriptions upon the part that hangs over the edge. Such quilts as these are mostly intended for use in hospital wards and infirmaries.'*

Members of the church or chapel did what they could to raise sufficient funds for the building work. The sewing groups made quilts, which were sold, often by auction to the highest bidder. The chapels would not raffle their quilts as this would have been looked upon as gambling, not at all appropriate for a chapel group! Whether the quilts were intended for home use or for use in hospitals, we may never know.

Sometimes called *"Bible", "Scripture", "Hymn",* or even *"Hospital"* quilts, these examples incorporated ready printed texts, biblical quotations and hymns, on squares and rectangles of cotton, which were then stitched together, in a form so that they could be read! In 1882, **The Girl's Own Paper** featured an article entitled *A Chat about Quilts.* The author writes, *' I shall endeavour to select such as I think not only the most novel and costly for home use, but those that will be found serviceable, pretty, and reasonable as gifts to hospitals and the poor.'* The quilts were used in hospital wards and sometimes were the work of soldiers, invalided out of war.

Rachel Nichols in her article *'Scripture Coverlets from Printed Blocks',* in **Quilt Studies 2004,** throws some light on the possible origin of these pieces, highlighting the work of Robert Mimpriss, born in 1797, well known for his Christian evangelism. Mimpriss was a regular contributor to such magazines as **The British Workman**, with his story of *The Patchwork Quilt.*

Making up one of Mr.Mimpriss's patchwork quilts from The British Workman. (28,300)

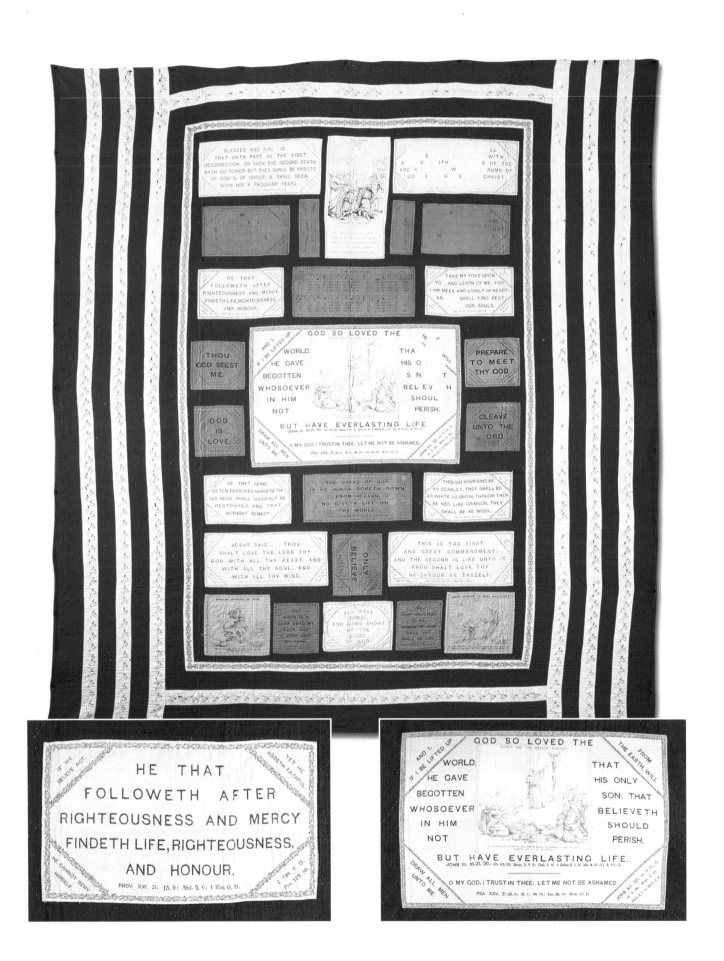

This quilt was made c.1870-1880 and although crudely quilted, illustrates well the use of printed texts, which have been machine appliquéd to a background of Turkey red twill material. (1986-42)

These chapel quilts are superb social documents, recording the chapel members of a particular area, and have even enabled individuals to build up family connections. They sometimes also record the names and dates of the ministers.

A Turkey red and white quilt, composed of triangles, with names carefully embroidered on, helped to complete the funding of the building of the Zion Chapel, Methodist New Connection, at Sheriff Hill, Gateshead in 1894. (1994-31)

This album coverlet is composed of Turkey red fabric in squares alternating with white squares, which have been machined together. Each square has been hand embroidered, with the signature of the chapel member, who had subscribed towards the making of the coverlet. This example was produced to raise funds for the Methodist Chapel in Lanchester, Co. Durham, and celebrates the Coronation of Edward VII in 1902. (1984-188)

The Birtley Primitive Methodist Church celebrated the completion of the funding of their building with their "Victory Quilt", in 1921.   (2002-78)

A most unusual coverlet, c. 1900-1920, consisting of embroidered panels of white cotton, joined together with lace, commemorates the Darlington Poor Law Union. (1993-236)

Wedding Quilts

In the North, a special quilt would be made for a girl's wedding, and sometimes indeed for a young man also. These quilts often featured designs and motifs such as hearts and baskets, which were recognised as symbols of love and fruitfulness.

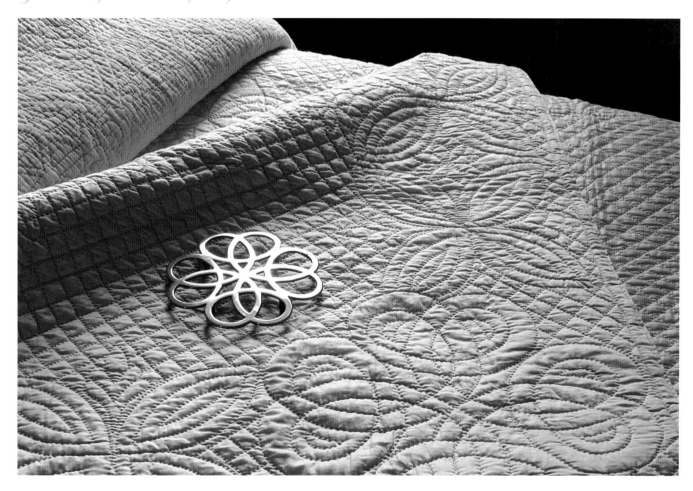

A FAVOURITE DESIGN was the *true lover's knot* that has no end, which has been used as a symbol for eternal love for centuries. This stitched pattern was often used in the centre and corners of a wedding quilt. A *cable* symbolised long life and therefore should not break of at the corners. Other gifts incorporating this motif were also made in the form of trivets and kitchen fenders, the same template being adaptable for several purposes!

This quilt shows clearly the blue pencil markings of a stamped quilt, and was probably a special order, to be sewn by Mary Jane Turnbull for her wedding at Leadgate, County Durham, in 1906, when she was 25 years old. (2001-41.1)

The Wedding Quilt.
Oil painting by Ralph Hedley, 1883.

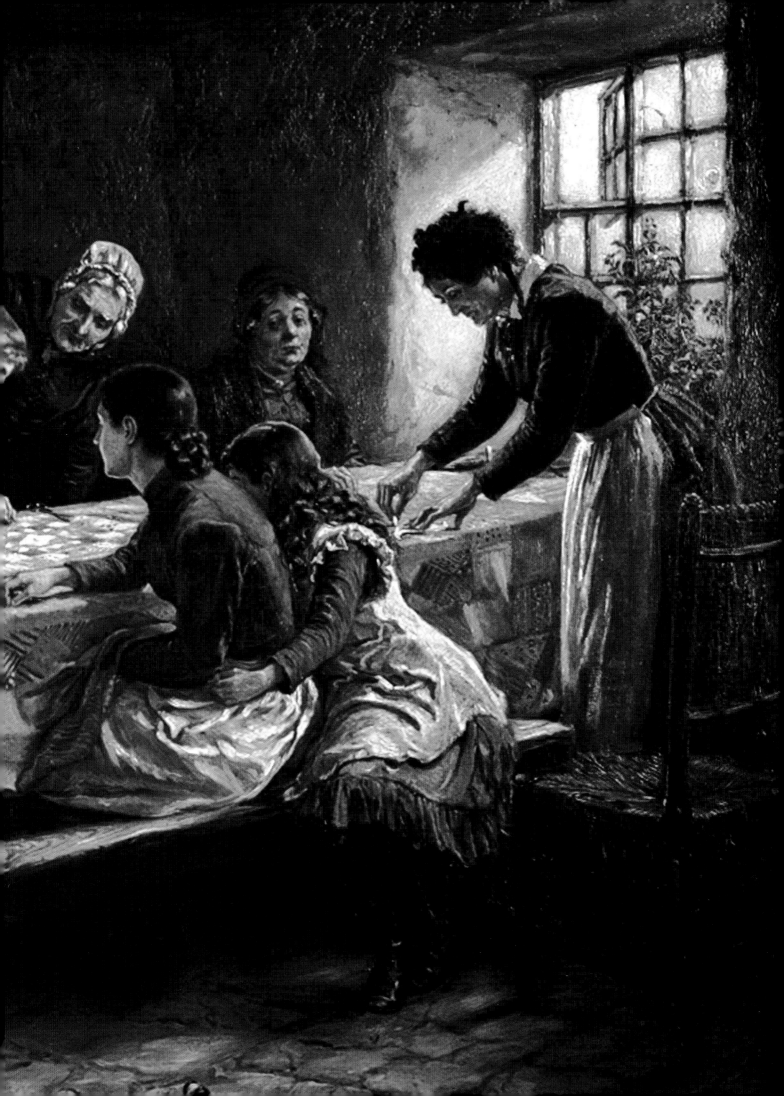

*A wedding quilt, c.1815-1830, from the Weardale area, in patchwork
with applied leaves, flowers and hearts. (1990-282)*

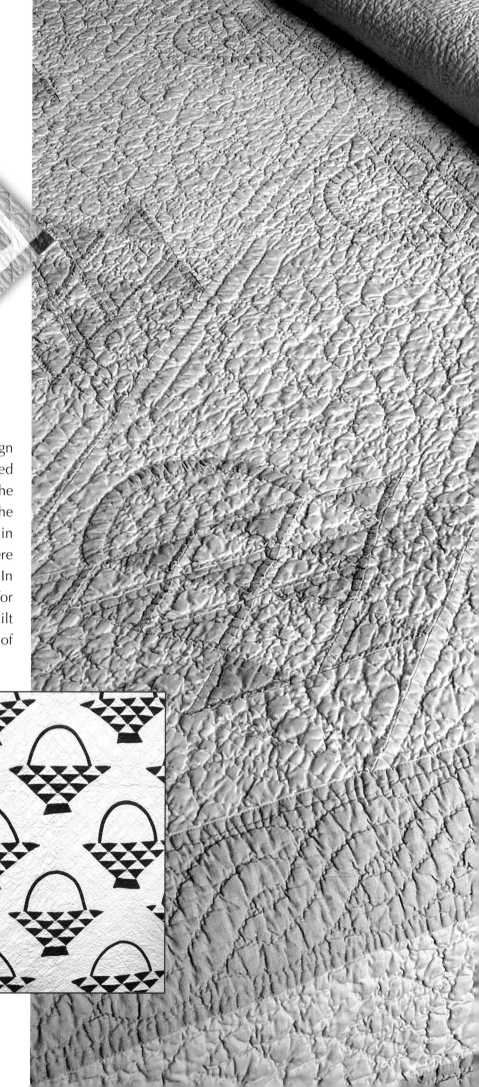

Baskets were a favourite patchwork design on wedding quilts, as they symbolised prosperity and fruitfulness. Normally the baskets themselves were pieced and the handles applied. The pattern was popular in America, especially on block quilts, where the pattern was repeated over the quilt. In some quilts, the basket motif was used for corners and as a centrepiece. This quilt (right) was made by Janey Middleton of Mickley, County Durham, c. 1920. (1985-336.1)

Detail from a patchwork and appliqué quilt in Turkey red and green cotton, made by Mrs. Isabella Cruddas of Rookhope, Weardale, c. 1870 - 1880. (above) (1984-70)

Detail from a Turkey red and white basket quilt, (right) made c.1880, in the Keswick area. The baskets have been pieced from triangles and the handles applied. The reverse is of white cotton. The quilting is very simply done in wineglass pattern. (1982-295)

Very fine chintz wedding quilt,
both sides shown here, made from
fabrics dating between 1840 and
1910. (1968-94)

A very fine quilt of cotton pieced squares, with brown printed border and reverse of white cotton. This quilt was made in Northumberland, most likely as a wedding present. The fabrics seem to span a period from c.1840 to the early 1900s. The overall pieced assembly is not a typical early arrangement. The quilting follows the squares. (1968-94)

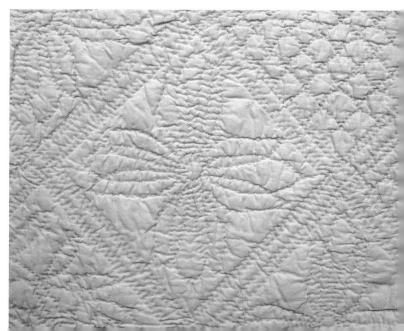

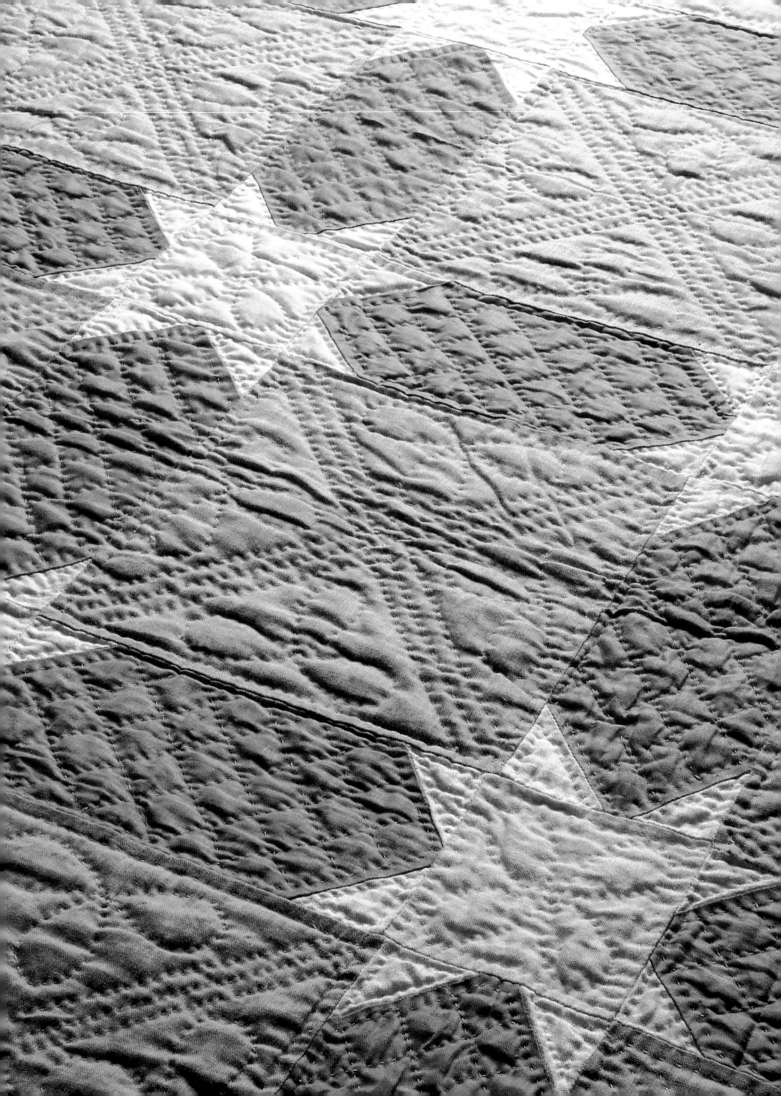

QUILT TYPES

During the 19th and 20th centuries, a wide variety of North Country quilts were produced. In the early years of the 19th century, the framed patchwork quilt, sometimes known as a medallion quilt, predominated.

A MERICAN INFLUENCES crept in from the 1850s and pieced block quilts became popular. Strippy quilts were known in the North from 1830, though they were usually later in date. From the 1850s, increasing numbers of wholecloth quilts were produced in the North. These wholecloth quilts are often called "Durham" quilts, but in fact many of them were made in Northumberland, so "North Country" would be a more appropriate description. All types of quilts were produced throughout the North East of England.

*Detail (left) block pieced star quilt
c. 1900-10, from Weardale. (1993-178)*

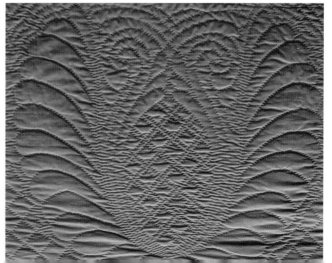

Wholecloth Quilts

Detail of "stamped" quilt in the Allenheads style. The blue pencil markings highlight the design of the radiating leaves and roses. (1972-658.129)

A wholecloth quilt consists of one piece of fabric, the strips of which are seamed together to form the quilt top. The underside is usually made of a similar type of fabric, either in the same material or in a contrasting colour. The design is created by the pattern of stitches, which hold together the two layers of material, with a layer of wadding in between. The quilt top is marked or "stamped" with the pattern, before the quilt is put into the quilt frame ready for stitching.

IN MOST CASES the design on a wholecloth quilt consists of a central design and corner designs, with a border pattern or borders around the outer edge. The rest of the quilt is quilted with an infill pattern such as *diamond* or *wineglass*. Sometimes the quilt is quilted in strips and may well have been marked in the frame. Alternatively an overall repeat pattern is used.

Wholecloth quilts are sometimes made from homespun wool, though more often than not, they are made from cotton or cotton sateen, known as Roman sateen. Pure silk is used for the best quilts. From the 1930s onwards, man-made fabrics such as rayon satin and crepe de chine, came into fashion and a number of quilters preferred to use these shinier fabrics, which they felt showed off their stitching to better advantage.

Detail of wholecloth homespun wool quilt, (left) quilted in strips (1990-101.3)

Cream cotton sateen quilt illustrating the style of George Gardiner's work. The quilt is known to have been "stamped" in Allenheads in 1903. The central *rose* with radiating *leaves, feathers* and *roses*, and elaborate freely drawn corner design, with *Prince of Wales feathers* and *hammock* border, are typical of his work. The quilting was completed in 1921 by Mrs. HARRIET ADAMSON, of Rookhope, the wife of George Adamson, an engineer in the local leadmines.

(1963-58)

Cream cotton sateen quilt in the Allenheads style. The design conforms to George Gardiner's type, with its central *rose, feathers* and *leaves* radiating from the centre. The outer *hammock* border, with its flowing corner design is also very typical Allenheads work. The skill and accuracy of the marking, particularly of the *diamond* infill, is a trademark of these professionally drawn quilts. This quilt was one of a number, to have come from the house of an old lady, originally from the Haydon Bridge area.

(1972-658.118)

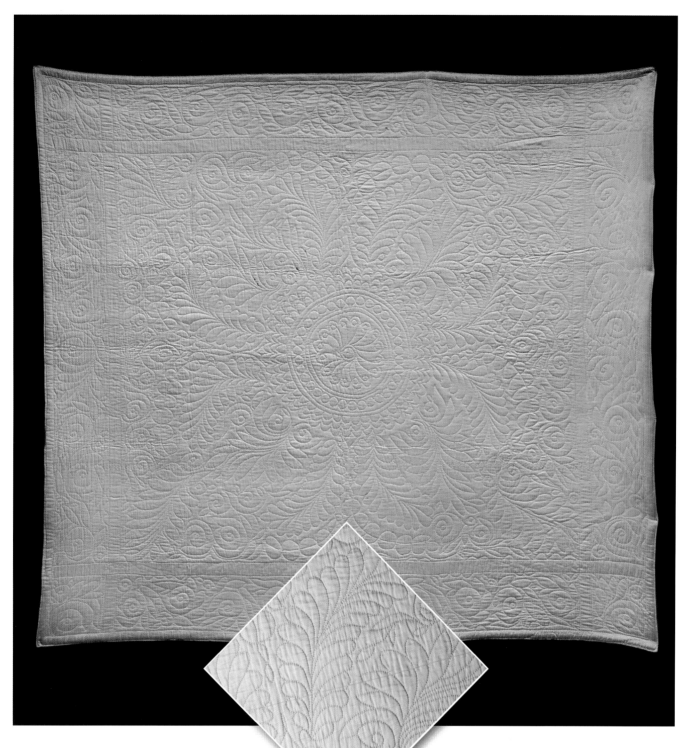

Gold cotton sateen quilt with a reverse of green satin. The green satin was obviously the material in fashion at the time of making, though sadly it has not worn as well as the cotton sateen! The quilt is very well designed with a large and elaborate central pattern of *leaves* and *feathers* radiating from a central *rose*. A more unusual double lined straight outer border encloses a *scroll* or *coxcomb* design. The quilt was made in 1939 by Mrs. MARY POTTS of Chester-le-Street, County Durham. Mary was a widow who earned her living by quilting. (1972-555)

Green cotton sateen quilt, with reverse of pink cotton sateen. A rather formal and geometric design, with its rigid square borders, this quilt seems to have more in common with the Welsh tradition, though favourite North Country patterns of *running feather* and *roses* have been used, with *fans* graduating in size from the outer to the inner borders. The quilting is quite finely undertaken though the outer frill is less characteristic. The quilt was made in Neville's Cross, Durham c. 1900. (1978-946)

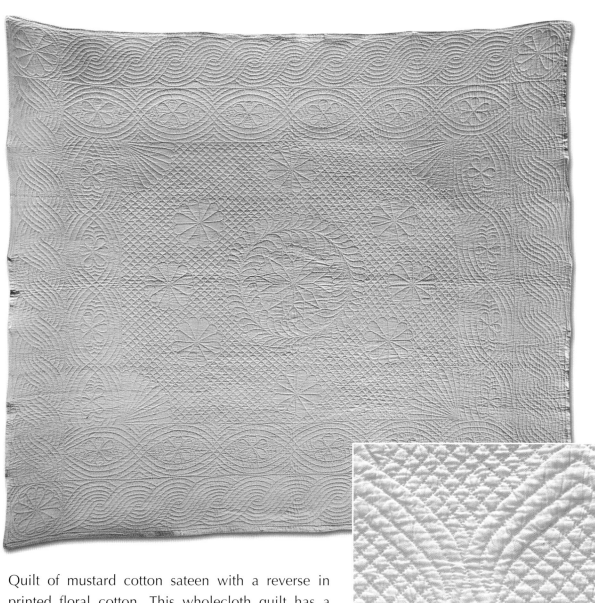

Quilt of mustard cotton sateen with a reverse in printed floral cotton. This wholecloth quilt has a simple pleasing design of eight *roses* around a *feather circle* enclosing a *star*. There is an outer border of *twist/cable* with *roses* in each corner, which indicates that the quilt was made by a less experienced quilter, not wishing to turn the corner in the *cable* design. An inner *trail* border is set on *diamond* infill. The quilt was made in Crook, County Durham, c.1910. (1971-241)

Wholecloth quilt in white cotton with overall pattern of *hay spade*. The quilt was made in 1920, by Mrs. A. IRELAND, a farmers's wife of Thornaby on Tees (1972-4).

Quilt of pink cotton sateen with reverse in white cotton sateen. The quilt has an unusual outer border of *whorls* and *scrolls*. The corner designs are composed of an urn with *scrolls* and *leaves* radiating towards the centre, which is made up of *running feather* and *leaf* in a *diamond* shape. *Diamond* infill is used for the background overall. The quilt was probably made in the 1930s in Castleside, County Durham, by Mrs. PHOEBE ENGLISH (born in Castleside in 1870), assisted by her niece Mrs. Nancy Lister (born in 1903). Both ladies were expert quilters and spent much time together. This quilt is very similar in design to 2001-33, which also came from Castleside. The same person may have designed both quilts. (2006-167)

A quilt of peach cotton sateen with reverse of yellow cotton sateen. The design is very individual to Mrs. SHEPHERD, a miner's wife from Amble in Northumberland. Her mother, who came from Coquet Island probably influenced her in her choice of design. The outer border is carefully worked with large *shells* and the corner design taken *'from the seat of a bentwood chair'*. Although Mrs. Shepherd ran quilting clubs, this quilt was made in 1935, for her son's "bottom drawer", but, as he never married, it came to the museum instead! (1980-744)

LOVE
ONE ANOTHER

BEAUTY and the BEAST

D. FRED' TAY

Illustration from The Graphic Issue 1882, entitled 'Christmas comes but once a year' - a scene at Evelina Hospital, from a painting by C. J. Staniland. Note the strippy quilt on the bed. These quilts were often made to be presented to hospitals to brighten up the wards. (168.302)

Strippy Quilts

The strippy quilt is constructed using strips of fabric, stitched together, usually running lengthways. Two contrasting fabrics normally of the same width are used, a very popular combination being Turkey red and white.

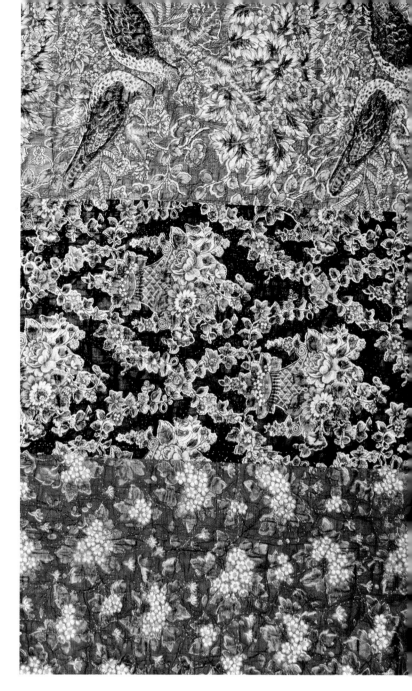

SOMETIMES printed fabrics and pastel shades provide variety, particularly in quilts of the early 1900s. Occasionally broad and narrow strips are used together. Other variations include zig zag strips with an outer border, and strip quilts pieced within the strip.

The quilting designs usually correspond to the strips though sometimes they run across the strips. In many cases the strips are marked out and quilted in the frame with designs appropriate for border patterns such as the *twist, plait, cable, feather, twist* and *running diamond*. A central motif demands more design skills from the quilter, but can occasionally be seen on some strip quilts.

Strippy quilts did tend to be the quilts made for everyday usage.

Most surviving strippy quilts are from the 1850 – 1930 period. This quilt dates to the 1830s period and is probably one of the earliest known strippy quilts to survive. It is composed of three different block printed chintzes with an underside of white calico. The chintzes are of a floral basket on a dark indigo background, a floral design on a drab background and a pheasant and tree design on a light green background. The quilting does not follow the strips. The quilt came from Barrasford in Northumberland and had been passed down in the family. This piece was certainly not a working class quilt! (1963-526)

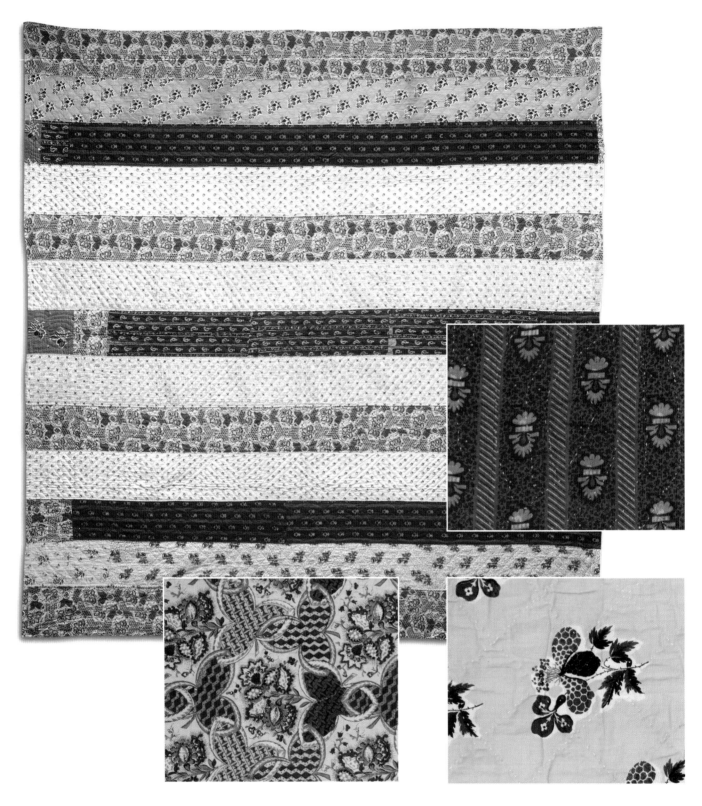

Strippy quilt consisting of early cotton chintzes with a reverse of cream calico. The quilting follows the strips in *zig-zag, small diamond* and *twist*. The quilt has been pieced and patched within the strips. The strip of chrome yellow cotton is typical of the 1820s/30s period and the other fabrics probably date to the 1830s. The quilt came from Dinnington, near Newcastle upon Tyne, and is c. 1840. (1970-90.7)

Blue and pink printed strip quilt, with reverse of white cotton. The quilting follows the strips, though unusually the patterns are not symmetrical. The quilt was made by Mrs. PHILLIPSON of Rispby, near Rookhope in Weardale, of pre 1855. (1972-138)

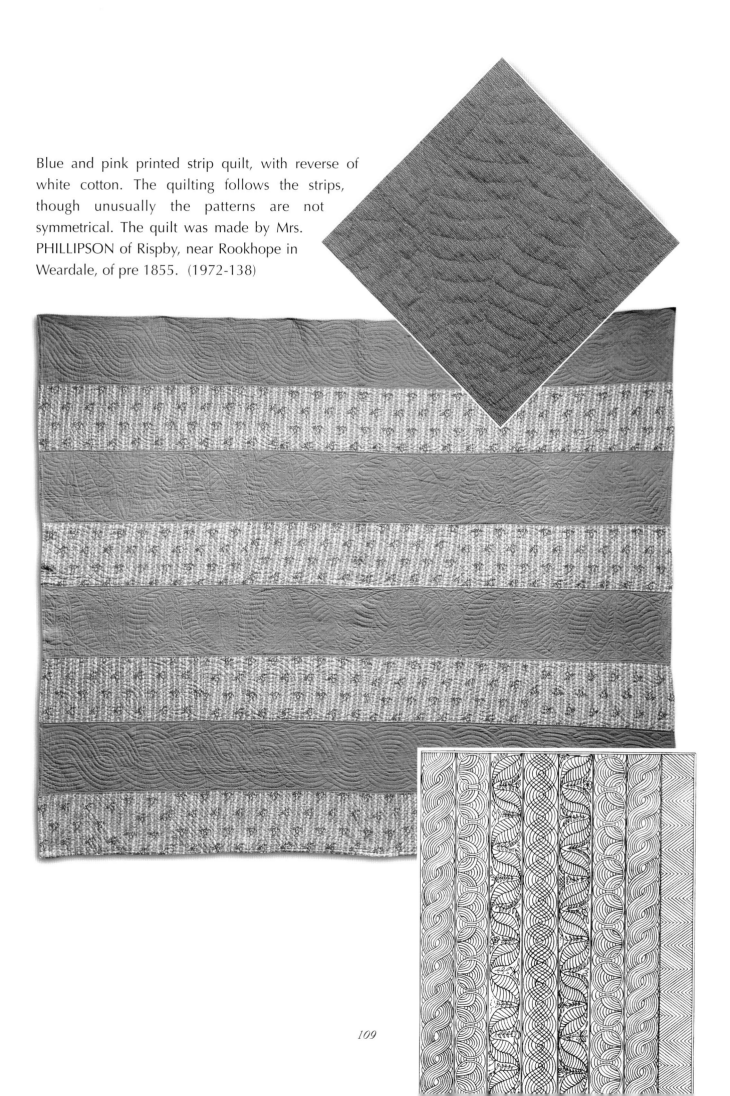

Mustard and cream cotton sateen strippy with reverse in dark pink sateen. The quilting, in *running diamond, fan, rose* and *feather hammock*, follows the strips, but also carries across them.

The quilt was made in 1899, probably as a wedding present, by the donor's grandmother's sister, ISABELLA CALVERT, of Thornley, Co. Durham. (1978-709.1)

Few strippy quilts seem to have survived illustrating the stamped blue pencil design. Here it can be seen to perfection, the pattern having been very professionally drawn onto the quilt, though the design is unusual, and possibly very personal to the maker. The quilt was made by SARAH HUNTER WALKER of Annfield Plain, Co. Durham, c.1930. Sarah was the fourth daughter of Thomas Walker, a miner, and she worked at the Annfield Plain Co-op Store. Her great grandfather was a blacksmith and some of her family worked with horses, which may account for the *horseshoe* pattern. (2006-146.1)

Turkey red and white strippy quilt, with reverse of white cotton. The fine quilting follows the strips in a *running feather* design and *running diamonds* enclosing a *rose, fan* and *leaf* pattern. The quilt was made c.1870-1880, by a lady from Slaley in Northumberland, who ran quilting clubs. The quilt had been made for the wedding of the donor's husband's parents. Mrs. Nixon said *'When I came here 64 years ago (1908) my late husband showed it to me and said it had not to be used'*. (1972-97)

This quilt, in the popular Turkey red and white cotton, with a reverse of white cotton, consists of five red and four white strips. The quilting is unusual in that it does not follow the strips but has a central motif of a *true lover's knot* surrounded by a *wineglass* pattern and outer borders of *trail, running feather* and *leaf* patterns. The quilt came from the West Cornforth in County Durham and was made c. 1870. (1962-143)

A more unusual strippy quilt made up of strips of pink and white check shirting with contrasting blue and white shirting. The strips are quilted in *wave, worm, fan* and *hammock*, following the strips. The quilt was made by ELIZABETH TEESDALE, (1873-1919) of Riggside, St.John's Chapel, Weardale, c. 1890. The quilt had followed the family out to Canada, however in 2000, they decided it should come home! (2000-90.1)

Pieced strippy quilt, combining pastel cotton printed squares with Turkey red cotton squares, within the strips, giving a really vibrant effect. Quilting follows the strips in *twist, rose, running diamond* and *bellows*. The quilt was made, c.1890, by Miss SARAH EGGLESTONE, a well-known quilter and dressmaker from Westgate in Weardale, who died in 1959, aged 85 years. She made this quilt with her grandmother, *"Granny Lee". 'She was a wonderful quilter. Her fingers literally flew over the material'.* (1962-140)

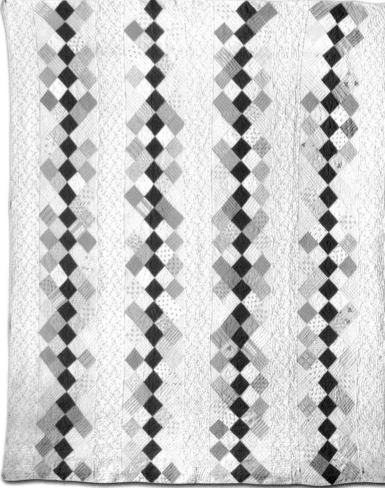

Pieced strippy quilt in pastel coloured printed cottons. The quilt is composed of pieced squares and triangles set into the strips. The colour scheme is very imaginative and appears deceptively modern.

The quilting is of fine quality and follows the strips in *twist* and *running diamond.* The quilt was collected from a Dr. Barnardo shop in the Consett area of County Durham. A rarity indeed, this quilt is signed and dated on the reverse Oct 24th 1877. (1980-693)

Patchwork and Applique Quilts

There has always been a strong tradition of patchwork or piecing, as it is sometimes known, in the North Country. In the 18th and 19th centuries patchwork predominates and this is well exemplified by the number of patchwork quilts in the collections at Beamish. Both patchwork and appliqué are extremely ancient crafts: patchwork involves the sewing together of shapes of material, and appliqué consists of their application to the surface of the main fabric.

"A Snapper-up of unconsider'd Trifles."
Winter's Tale.

London Published for the Proprietor at Mess.rs Rowe & Walters, 49 Fleet St. Dec.r 1824

THE EARLIEST KNOWN, though undated, English patchwork is at Levens Hall, near Kendal, reputedly made, c.1708 from pieces of imported Indian prints. Patchwork in the 18th century was usually in silk, the earliest dated known patchwork is the 1718 silk patchwork coverlet in the collection of the Quilters' Guild of the British Isles. Recent research has shown that patchwork, quilting and appliqué should not be regarded just as thrift crafts, worked in a climate of poverty. Often items, particularly during the early 1800s, were worked because they were fashionable crafts of the time.

The paper templates would be removed when the piecing was complete. In some cases, unfinished quilts and coverlets have been discovered with all their papers still intact, making for the most exciting reading of cuttings, providing a social background, and documentary evidence, which otherwise would be lost.

It is unusual to find quilts and coverlets in appliqué prior to 1800. Although the technique may well have been used for repairs, it did not generally become popular as a technique until after 1840, when it was often combined with patchwork.

In later years, economy provided the stimulus for patchwork, which developed into a craft of its own. Much patchwork is unquilted, or the quilting, if it does exist, is secondary in importance to the patchwork. Cloth of all kinds was used from the mid to late 19th and early 20th centuries. Cotton dress prints were used a great deal and these would include floral designs, small spot prints and chintzes. Wool was also used in the upland areas, where the mills would provide sample pieces and "fents". One of the main sources of patchwork pieces, was from remnants and left overs from furnishing and dressmaking.

At this period, printed cotton fabric was regarded as a prestige material, and was often purchased especially for working in patchwork. Most English patchwork consisted of a method known as mosaic patchwork, which involved piecing over papers. This was considered to be the most accurate method, and although very time consuming, could be used for elaborate designs successfully.

Victorian print (above) illustrating wicker crib with patchwork quilt (165,221)

This framed quilt illustrates well the use of early 1800s printed cotton fabrics and printed centrepiece.
The quilt was probably made in Teesdale and dates to the late 1820s/ early 1830s.
(1989-395)

Patterns usually consist of one of three types: - a framed or medallion design, a design pieced from blocks, or an all over design. From the mid eighteenth century until the early 1900s, quilted patchwork would have been a familiar sight, not only in farmhouses and cottages.

The framed or medallion quilt, as it is sometimes known, consists of a central motif, surrounded by a series of frames or borders. The borders are often pieced and sometimes feature applied work within the border, or can be of a single fabric; they can also vary in width, reducing towards the centre.

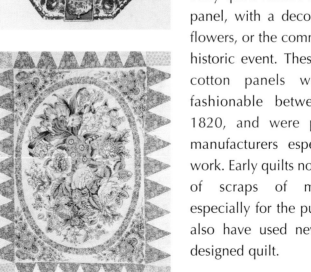

This is one of the oldest styles to be used in patchwork quilts, and is particularly typical of the quilts made in the early 1800s, throughout the British Isles. Sometimes these early quilts feature a central printed panel, with a decorative basket of flowers, or the commemoration of a historic event. These block printed cotton panels were especially fashionable between 1800 and 1820, and were printed by the manufacturers especially for this work. Early quilts not only made use of scraps of material saved especially for the purpose, but may also have used new fabrics for a designed quilt.

Centrepiece with Princes Charlotte of Wales married to Leopold Prince of Saxe Coburg May 2 1816 (above centre)

Patchwork and appliqué quilt, in printed cottons, with reverse in white cotton. The quilt is pieced overall in blocks of squares and triangles. Alternating squares demonstrate well the technique of "broderie perse", where individual motifs have been cut out from the printed fabrics and applied to the white cotton background forming a cohesive design.

Hearts and trees of life predominate in the central squares. The outer corners have an assortment of irregular shapes and these squares would seem to have been trimmed at some stage. The fabrics appear to date back to the 1840s, which might imply that although the quilt has on it a date of 1839, it may well not have been made until the 1850s. (2006-206)

The central panel of the quilt bears, in embroidery, the words " J. A. Blenkinsop. Born on the 2 of June in the Year 1839 ad. " Research shows that Jane Ann Blenkinsop, was christened on 12th July 1839 at St. Thomas', Stockton on Tees. It may well be that the quilt was made by the lady herself, though at a date later than 1839, which would accord with the dates of the fabrics used. (2006-206)

Framed or medallion quilt of printed cottons in muted colours. The quilt is cleverly composed of pieced squares and triangles, which form the borders in ever decreasing widths towards the centre panel. The quilt was made c.1850, by the donor's mother's aunt, who lived in Carlisle, Cumberland. (1977-993.2)

A very typical arrangement of a framed quilt of multi-coloured printed cottons with central chequerboard of Turkey red and white. Set into the corners are squares of blue fabric. The quilting follows the pieced design in *trail, diamond* and *plait*. The quilt probably dates c. 1870. (1971-16.11)

Framed quilt of brightly coloured printed cottons, with central square offset as diamond. The quilting follows the pieced work in a *rose* centre with *zigzag twist* and *diamond* infill. The quilt includes some quite early fabrics, though probably dates c.1870/1880 and comes from County Durham. (1967-894)

Framed quilt, c. 1815-1860, combining some early fabrics. The reverse is of white cotton. The centre square encloses 25 pieced stars, surrounded by borders made up of pieced strips and rectangles set at an angle, in a T shape. The quilt is quilted overall in a *wineglass* pattern.

(1977-1244)

A similar framed quilt of c.1865, of printed cottons in beige, browns, cream and gold. Some fabrics may date to the early 1800s, some 1820s and some mid 1840s. The central square encloses 9 pieced squares surrounded by strips of pieced squares. An outer border of *Wild Goose Chase* pieced design links the corner squares. Quilting is in *wineglass* overall.

(1977-1262)

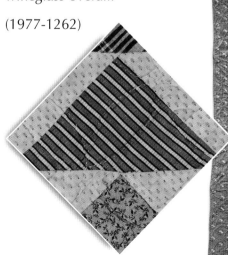

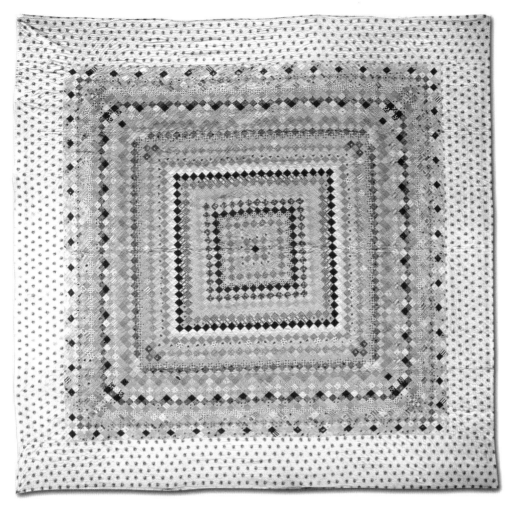

Pieced medallion quilt composed of tiny squares of printed cottons. The use of Turkey red squares, emphasises the framed construction. The outer borders are quilted in *hammock* and the central circle encloses a design of eight *leaves*. The quilt dates about 1870 and is from Newcastle upon Tyne.

(1973-518)

Medallion quilt of printed cottons with an unusual Turkey red bias edging to the squares. The quilting is in a *diamond* and *leaf* pattern. Mrs. Elizabeth Robinson, of Newcastle upon Tyne made the quilt for her daughter's "bottom drawer" in 1907.

(1982-227)

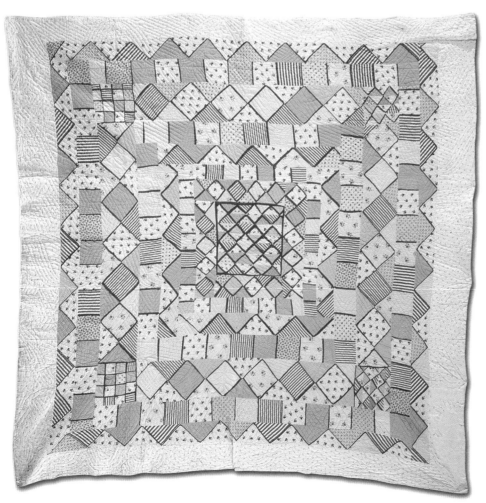

Medallion quilt of multi-coloured printed cottons, in floral designs. The borders are composed of pieced squares and triangles around a central square enclosing a wind mill design. The quilting runs overall in a *diamond* pattern, the emphasis being on the pierced work rather than on the quilting. The quilt was acquired from a farm sale at Thornton Rust, near Askrigg, North Yorkshire and was made about 1870- 1880.

(1982-227)

Medallion quilt of printed cottons. An eight-pointed star on a white background is set into a series of pieced borders of squares and triangles. The quilting consists of a *feather circle*, with an outer *twist* border, and an inner border of *running feather* enclosing *wineglass* infill. The quilt came from the Kirby Thore area of Westmorland and was made by the donor's great grandmother before 1890.

(1972-210.42.2)

A variation on the framed quilt can be seen here. The patchwork design is bold, with its centrepiece, around which are arranged a series of Turkey red and white borders. Quilting overall is in *wave* or *zigzag* pattern. The quilt was made, about 1870, in the Kirkby Stephen area of Westmorland, where greater emphasis tended to be placed on the pieced design rather than on fine and decorative quilting. (1982-296)

Mrs. Goldsborough of Pelton, County Durham, made this striking Turkey red and white cotton appliqué quilt, for the wedding of Isabella Levitt in 1895. The quilt has been embroidered with the initials IL. The pieced stars and leaves have been applied by machine, though the quilt is hand stitched in strips of *fan, flowers, running feather, worm* and *plait,* across the entire quilt, not following the patchwork. The reverse is of white cotton. The bold use of Turkey red and white is typically northern.

(1976-821.4)

A particularly fine North Country example of patchwork and appliqué in the distinctive colour scheme of Turkey red printed cotton with contrasting green on a white background. The baskets are unlike any others found at this period and may well have been copied or influenced by work of the early 1800s. The alternating borders are typical of the North Country, although the overall arrangement seems to owe something to American designs. The quilting follows the patchwork design with a *diamond* pattern on all the panels, the centre having a border of *roses* and each strip being quilted in *worm* and *chain*. The quilt was made by Isabella Cruddas of Rookhope in Weardale c. 1870-80. (1984-70)

The *"basket"* was a very old and well-used pattern for pieced work, usually made from triangles, the handle being applied to the top of the basket. Mary Ann Shanks of Benwell, Newcastle upon Tyne, made this naïve quilt in brilliantly coloured flannels and suitings, c.1910. The quilt is quite heavy and the filling may well be an old blanket. The reverse is in plain wool. The quilt may well have been made for a wedding, however the patchwork and quilting are both rather crude even though the overall design is bold and imaginative. The overall effect is most pleasing, due to the bright colour combination. (1973-517)

A fine framed or medallion quilt *(left)* in pink, blue, beige and white cotton fabrics, this quilt is designed around a central pieced rose with smaller flower sprigs attached. Set into the corners are other pieced roses with alternating borders, composed of triangles and zigzag patterns. The quilt was made c. 1890, by a member of the Thompson family, who farmed in Hexhamshire, Northumberland. (1999-58.1)

A particularly northern type of framed quilt was the pattern, which has come to be known as the *"Sanderson Star"*. A number of these survive usually in two contrasting colours; the design of alternating borders set around an eight pointed star is immediately recognisable as the work of Elizabeth Sanderson or one of her pupils. This example was probably made in Allenheads c. 1890-1900. It is of white cotton with a reverse of white cotton sateen indicating that there may well have been an interval between stamping and sewing. (1985-148)

This patchwork and appliqué quilt of c.1870, from Great Lumley, in County Durham, must have been stunning when first made. It is now sadly faded. It does, however, illustrate an imaginative use of Turkey red, green and orange on a white background, which was so popular in the northern counties. The reverse is of printed cotton. Smaller clusters, enclosed by a border of *Wild Goose Chase,* surround nine appliqué flowers in red. The fine quilting follows the pieced design. (1978-1029.1)

Mrs. MORPHET of Kirkby Stephen made this somewhat faded quilt, c. 1912. It has had a striking colour scheme of Turkey red, green and white, with an outer pieced border, and reverse of white cotton.

The quilting is very simply done in an overall *wave* pattern, as one would expect from this area. (1982-118)

Block quilts are generally constructed from a number of patchwork or appliquéd sections, usually in squares, which are then stitched together to form the quilt top. Many American quilts are made in this way, and although this method has come to be regarded as distinctively American, it has been used traditionally in the North of England for many years. There are numerous designs for block quilts, often combining two contrasting colours.

This quilt of Turkey red and white appliqué quilt in cotton, has a pieced block construction. The pattern is a variation of *Drunkard's Path,* however the pattern seems to have gone slightly awry! The reverse is of white cotton. The outer border has been machine appliquéd, though the quilt has been hand stitched in strips of *diamond, flower* and *wineglass* pattern. The quilt belonged to the grandmother of an old lady from Burnopfield, County Durham and was probably made c.1870-1880. (1986-293)

This block quilt combines printed and plain cottons, and its design of plain and pieced squares of *Irish Chain,* set diagonally and forming an overlaying grid pattern, is very effective. The reverse is of white cotton. The quilted design is of *diamonds* and *leaves.* The quilt, c.1880, came from Barnard Castle, County Durham. (1967-920.1)

The *Irish Chain* was a very popular patchwork pattern, on both sides of the Atlantic, though there is no evidence that it ever originated in Ireland. The pattern has been used since the 18th century and a number of versions are to be found, including single, double and even triple *Irish Chain*, according to the different methods of piecing the squares.

The inset shows a detail from a quilt in *Irish Chain.* The single chain has been made up in a mauve printed cotton fabric set on a white background. It is finely quilted with a diamond pattern enclosed in a circle. The quilt was made c.1870-1880 and came from Castleside, County Durham. (2004-19.2)

The four patch *Irish Chain* or *Double Irish Chain,* as it was called, was probably the best-known variant of this pattern. Here Turkey red, green and white have been used, with a reverse in white cotton. The quilting is very fine in an overall *diamond* pattern. The quilt was made c.1890 and came from North Shields. (1968-166.1)

The inset shows a detail from a quilt made in Northumberland, c.1870. A single *Irish Chain* quilt, with slight variation in the pattern is illustrated. The reverse is of white cotton and some fine quilting follows the patchwork in *rose* design, alternately on the red and white squares. (1983-234)

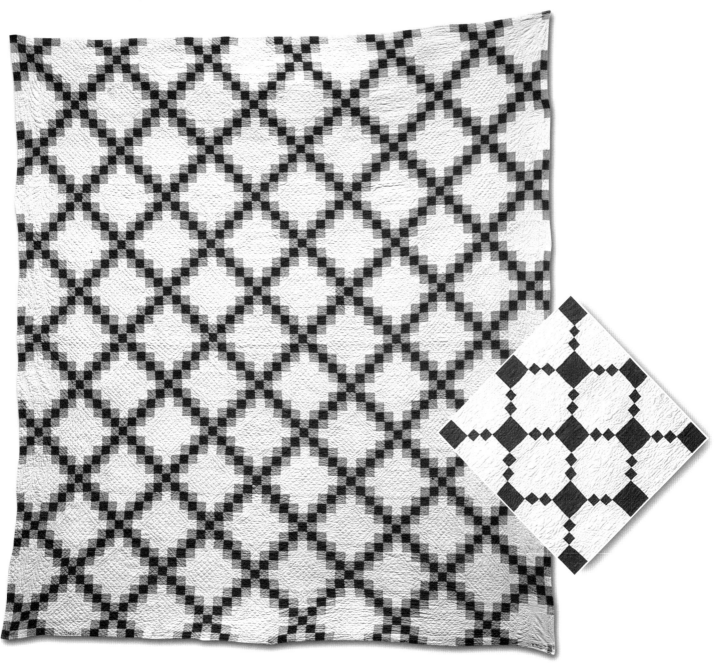

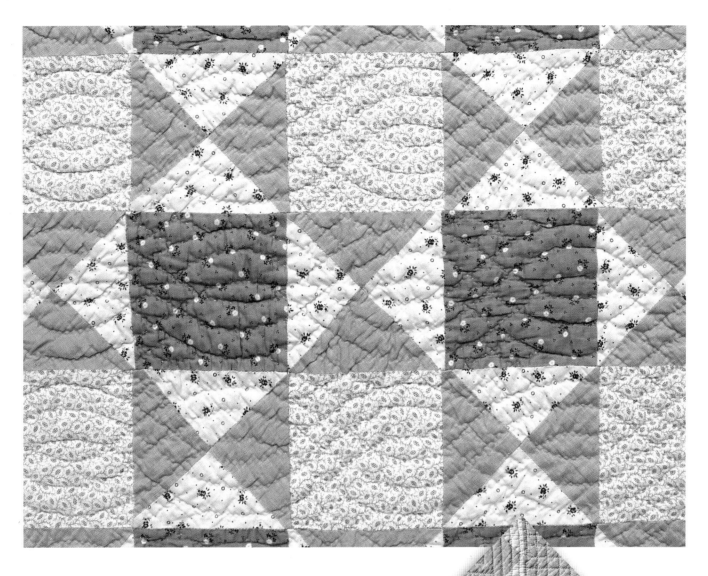

This cot quilt in pink, mauve and beige printed cottons has been pieced in blocks of triangles and squares. The reverse is of plain pink cotton and it is quilted overall in *trail*. Mrs. JANE BURNEY of Mickleton in Teesdale made the quilt for her grand daughter, Amy Jane Smith, in 1895. (1985-356.4)

Detail of a similarly constructed block patchwork quilt, also made by Mrs. Jane Burney of Mickleton, Teesdale, for her grand daughter's wedding in 1924. (1985-356.1)

Pieced block quilt of green and white cotton, with green stars set on a white background and a green *zigzag* outer border. The reverse is of white cotton. The quilting is extremely fine. It follows the pieced design in *diamond infill* and *leaves* on the white square blocks. The quilt came from the home of Mrs. Reed, whose family were grocers in Pity Me, Durham and it was probably made c. 1880. (1986-259)

Pieced block quilt in pink, blue and white cotton. The white stars are cleverly pieced into pink borders set onto the blue background. Note how the triangles forming the stars are all of different sizes and shapes made to fit. The quilting follows the patchwork in *diamond* and *rose*. It was probably made in Weardale c. 1890-1900. (1993-178)

Pieced block *Feathered Star* quilt in printed cotton chintz and white cotton with a white cotton reverse. The patchwork design consists of nine feathered stars evenly spaced across the quilt, with an inner saw tooth border, and an outer plain chintz border. The quilt has a rather more unusual pieced triangular edging. The quilting, which is of *rose* and *cross* with *diamond* infill overall, is of good quality, though it does not follow the patchwork. It is likely that this quilt came from the Allendale area and was made c.1890. (1971-16.2)

Starburst patchwork and appliqué quilt, of c. 1870, with brilliant colour combination of Turkey red, green, orange on a white background. The central red star is surrounded by circles of alternating pieced diamonds, with eight small pointed stars at each tip of the large star. The reverse is of white cotton. The stars are machine appliquéd to the white background, though the entire quilt is finely hand stitched. The quilt came from Weardale.

(1982-244)

Quilt of Turkey red, yellow and white cotton, with a reverse of Turkey red cotton. The quilt consists of a pieced *Starburst* pattern, composed of diamonds on a white background, with a red border. The quilt was made c.1920, by JANE HOLE, who came from a miner's family, in East Stanley, County Durham. Jane with her mother aand sister, made quilts for the family and also took part in the Women's Bright Hour at the West Pelton Methodist Chapel. (1994-202)

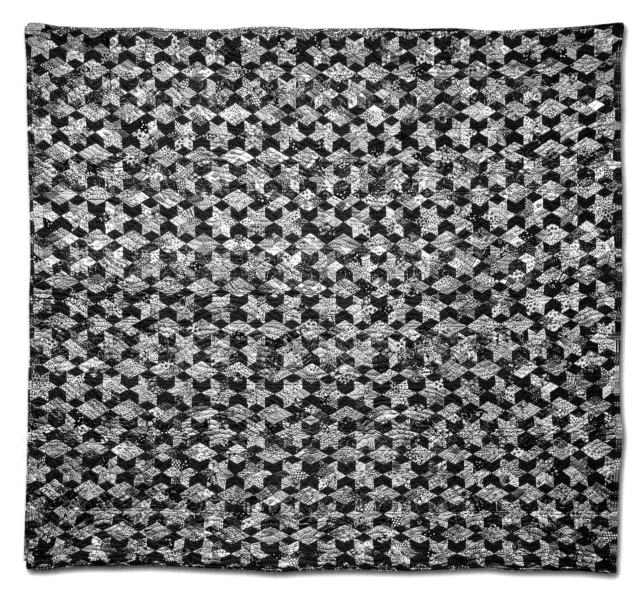

Patchwork quilt with an all over star design, in Turkey red and brightly printed cottons and white cotton reverse. The quilt is composed of small diamonds pieced to form stars and diamonds on a red background, and is quilted in strips of *worm* and *trail*. It was made, using 1930s fabrics, by ISABELLA WOMPHREY of Willington Quay, Newcastle upon Tyne. (1977-161.1)

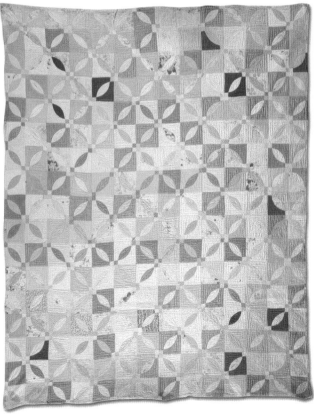

Pieced block quilt, in yellow, cream and green sateen, with some printed cotton fabric. The pieced design is a variation of *Robbing Peter to pay Paul*. The quilting follows the pieced pattern. The quilt was made, between 1907 and 1914, by Mrs. MATILDA CLISH, the wife of the Treasurer of Annfield Plain Co-operative Society. The fabrics would have been purchased from the Co-op, which may also have provided the quilt patterns. She made a quilt for each of her daughters, when they were married. (1981-365.1)

Family portrait of William and Matilda Clish and their family taken c.1897-1898

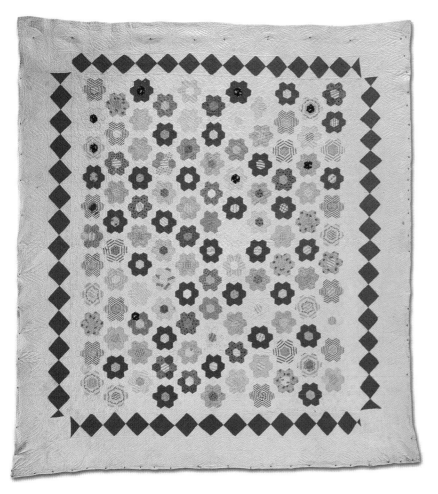

Quilts with an all over design are quite often composed of geometric shapes, such as pieced hexagons or squares, sometimes forming a honeycomb pattern. The hexagon, a typical English pattern had been known since the late eighteenth century. A favourite design, popular in the North East and Yorkshire, it was known as *Grandmother's Flower Garden*. These quilts sometimes consist of hundreds of tiny pieces, the more that were used, the better the quilt! So often, however, the concentration is on the pieced design and not the quilting. A number of pieced coverlets of this type survive unquilted.

Pieced all over quilt of printed cottons with Turkey red on a white cotton background, in *Grandmother's Flower Garden* pattern. The quilting follows the patchwork, and the quilt was made by Mrs. WALLACE of Beltingham, Bardon Mill, Northumberland c. 1850-60. (1979-795)

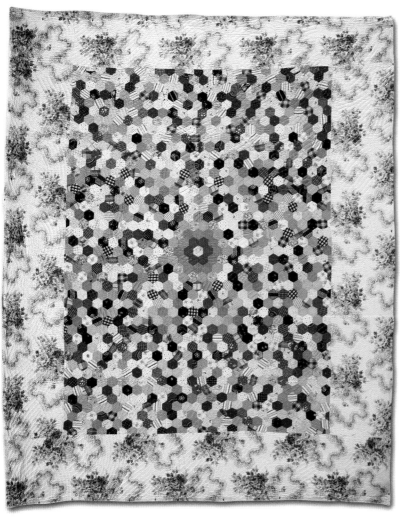

Pieced quilt of multi coloured cottons with printed floral cotton border. The quilt is composed of hexagons, in the *Grandmother's Flower Garden* pattern, and was made by RACHEL WADE, in about 1907. She was a dressmaker, from Seaton Burn, Newcastle upon Tyne, and made the quilt for her "bottom drawer", when she was 23 years old, however she was jilted and did not marry until she was 46 years old! (1985-221)

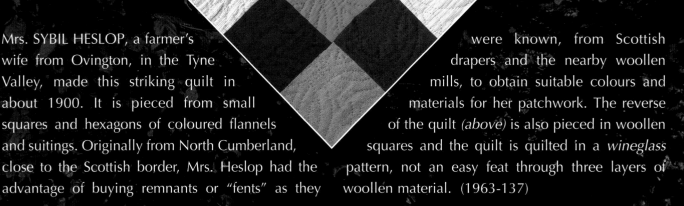

Mrs. SYBIL HESLOP, a farmer's wife from Ovington, in the Tyne Valley, made this striking quilt in about 1900. It is pieced from small squares and hexagons of coloured flannels and suitings. Originally from North Cumberland, close to the Scottish border, Mrs. Heslop had the advantage of buying remnants or "fents" as they were known, from Scottish drapers and the nearby woollen mills, to obtain suitable colours and materials for her patchwork. The reverse of the quilt *(above)* is also pieced in woollen squares and the quilt is quilted in a *wineglass* pattern, not an easy feat through three layers of woollen material. (1963-137)

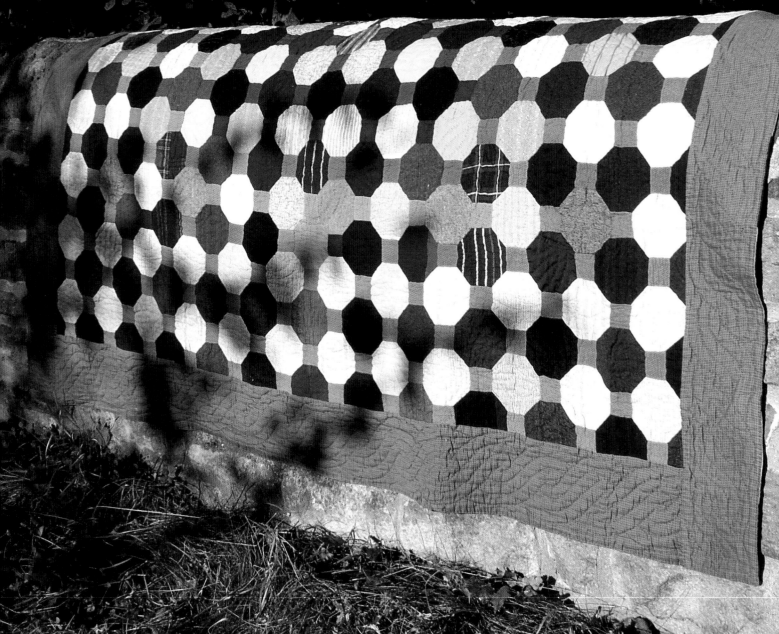

Mrs. Heslop also made this quilt, pieced from small squares of coloured flannels and suitings. It appears at first sight to be a rather haphazard design, however it has been carefully constructed and provides a very pleasing effect within a grid of black squares, quilted overall in a *wineglass* pattern. (1963-136)

Crazy coverlet in velvets, silks and satins, made about 1890, by Hannah Elizabeth Scott of Waldridge Fell. (1984-74.1)

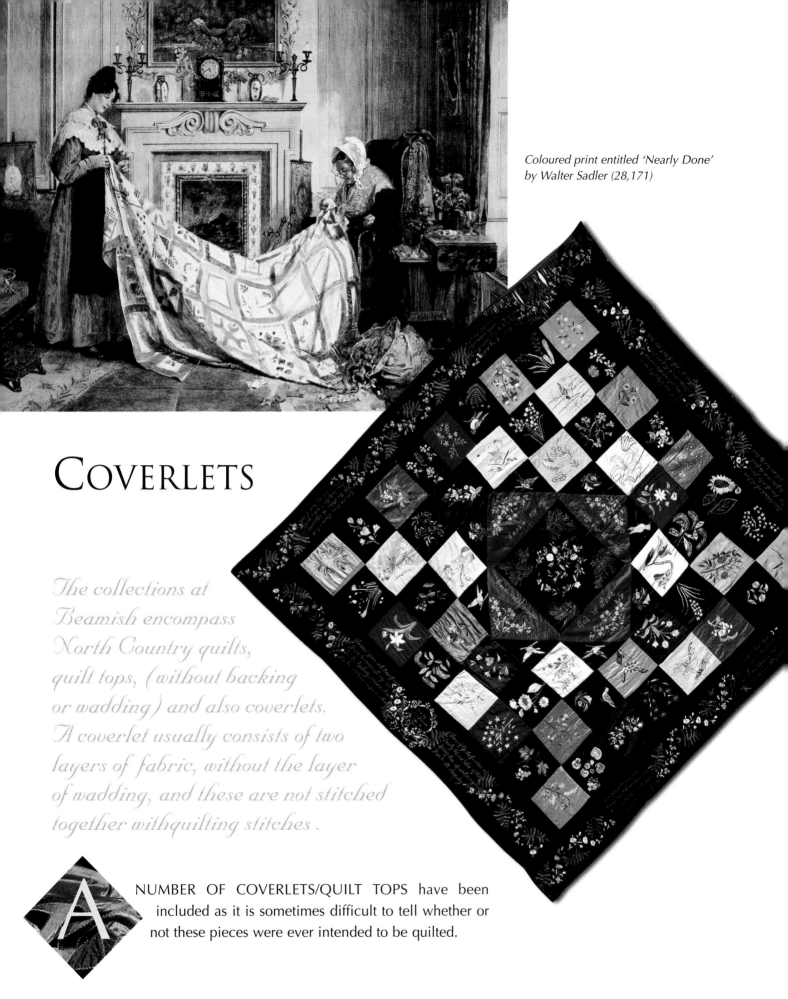

COVERLETS

The collections at
Beamish encompass
North Country quilts,
quilt tops, (without backing
or wadding) and also coverlets.
A coverlet usually consists of two
layers of fabric, without the layer
of wadding, and these are not stitched
together with quilting stitches .

A NUMBER OF COVERLETS/QUILT TOPS have been included as it is sometimes difficult to tell whether or not these pieces were ever intended to be quilted.

A wonderful example of a *Grandmother's Flower Garden* coverlet of tiny pieced hexagons in blocks of seven, on a white background. The coverlet is surrounded by borders of pieced triangles and pink cotton, these being the only sections which are quilted. The coverlet belonged to the donor's grandmother, Margaret Isabella Mitchell, who was born in 1833, and lived at Mossband Farm, Gretna Green. It was supposed to have been made in Northumberland prior to her marriage in 1856. (1967-939)

In this framed coverlet, MARY DICKINSON of Thornley, County Durham, used cut-out chintz appliqué, in natural leaf and flower shapes and combined them with geometrical pieced work to form the outer borders, in 1815. The coverlet also features hearts in the design and it is embroidered, in cross stitch, in the centre with the maker's name and date. It is likely that the materials were purchased especially for the coverlet. This piece came from the collection of Averil Colby, an authority on patchwork, whose books on the subject are well known. (1984-150)

An unfinished piece of patchwork, consisting of multi coloured printed cotton hexagons, surrounding clusters of white hexagons which are linked with small diamonds. The patchwork still retains all its original paper patterns of newspaper, some dating back to 1841 and 1855. The coverlet was made by "an elderly countrywoman" from Allenheads probably about 1860-70. (1971-129)

Pieced honeycomb coverlet of multi coloured printed cottons, with reverse of white cotton. This coverlet was made in Satley, County Durham in about 1870, though consists of a number of earlier fabrics. *(right)* (1972-640)

Coverlet of multi coloured cotton hexagons set on a white background with a reverse of white cotton. The reverse is marked 'Number of patches 7527. Date 1878'. The coverlet has an outer border of printed material, which is quilted in *twist*. It came from Riding Mill, Northumberland. *(bottom right)* (1971-371)

Honeycomb coverlet, made up of small hexagons joined by featherstitch, with reverse of white cotton. The coverlet was made, between 1966 and 1970, by Mrs. E. GARDNER of Carlton, near Richmond. *(below)* (1970-510)

This red and white coverlet, made of groups of gathered patches, joined by flat triangular patches, was made by Isabella Cruddas at Rookhope, Co. Durham, c.1860-70. It represents an unusual form of patchwork, where the pieces are tightly gathered by several running threads, attached to an interlining to hold them in place. Averil Colby made her own version of this coverlet in 1960.

(1988-315)

WALTER SCOTT, a Master Tailor, of Crookham village, in Northumberland, began this cot coverlet in 1872. Made from off cuts of suitings, it became rather too heavy for a child, and so work continued to enlarge it into a full size coverlet. Tweeds, wools and tartans, in the most elaborate shapes, have been appliquéd by machine, to create a really imaginative design. The medallion centre is made from uniform cloth. (1986-115)

This coverlet, pieced from squares of satinised cotton, and beautifully embroidered with various motifs, including butterflies, birds, snails and flowers, and also with the words of the hymn 'Jesu, lover of my soul', was made and signed in embroidery, by Ann Johnson, aged 78, of Hartlepool in 1883. (1973-273)

The later Victorian period saw a large number of quilts and coverlets, being produced in silks, satins and velvets, as dress fashions changed, allowing scraps of these fabrics to become available. Many of these were made, not for necessity, but to pass the time of day, as a leisure occupation, by those who could afford to employ servants to do the essential domestic chores.

This coverlet in satinised cotton, has been pieced in a lattice arrangement, of cotton strips, which have been appliquéd with stylised flowers and leaves, individually embroidered, giving a most attractive and delicate effect. The bold colour scheme and contrasting appliqué with outer trimming in lace, gives a very satisfactory result. The coverlet was made c. 1870 in Durham. (1972-629)

In the Victorian period, crazy patchwork was very much in vogue. Its construction did not require much skill, either in the planning or the stitching of the work. A dressmaker's rag bag was often a brilliant source for a wide variety of scraps of all kinds. The pieces would be laid onto a backing material and then stitched, often with herringbone stitching to give a more ornate effect. Most crazy work was unquilted.

In 1885, Weldon's **Practical Shilling Guide to Fancy Work**, gave full instructions for all the different types of patchwork. Crazy patchwork was sometimes known as Kaleidoscope or Japanese patchwork. Left overs of ribbons and velvets could be made into household furnishings, such as mantel piece trims, tea cosies and cushion covers as well as full size coverlets.

This crazy coverlet is made up of brilliantly coloured velvets, silks and satins, consisting of nine large pieced squares, incorporating a central eight pointed star, and outer pieced border of squares and triangles. The pieces are stitched with herringbone stitch and the corners of the triangles are embroidered. The coverlet was made by HANNAH ELIZABETH SCOTT of Waldridge Fell, Chester le Street, County Durham c.1890. (1984-74.1)

Detail of crazy coverlet in scraps of printed cotton. Even the smallest most misshapen pieces have been used to good effect. This coverlet was made c.1880 in the Whitley Bay area of Northumberland. (1978-884.2)

Patchwork reached a very high standard in its artistic quality in America, where the individual patterns of the early settlers, were given their own names, reflecting history, politics, religion and nature. Some of these patterns had been used in the North of England, *Log Cabin* being recognised as one of the earliest forms of patchwork. The pattern was used in a variety of ways to produce different effects, named in America as *Straight Furrow, Barn Raising* and *Pineapple*, to mention just a few.

The pattern is made up of strips of fabric, which can be worked equally satisfactorily in silks, velvets, cottons and wools. The arrangement of the strips, alternating in light and dark around a central square can produce some very different effects. This table centre, in silks, satins and velvets, was made by Mrs. EMMA CARLTON, of Amble, Northumberland, c.1900. (1988-239)

This Turkey red and white cotton, *Log Cabin* coverlet, using the colour contrast to create blocks of colour across the coverlet, came from Weardale, County Durham, and was probably made c.1900. (1997-75)

Log Cabin coverlet in wool and tweed fabrics, in a traditional arrangement. The coverlet was made by KATHERINE HUMPHREY of Wrekenton, Gateshead, in the 1930s, and the colour scheme does rather reflect the period. (1993-10)

The *Tumbling Box* or *Baby Blocks* pattern, is composed of three pieced diamonds, using carefully selected fabrics of contrasting colour in light, mid and dark tones, arranged to give a box effect. The pattern has been used for many years, though was extremely popular from 1870 to 1900, when fine silks were available to use. This example was made c. 1900. (1972-695)

Patterns & Templates

Quilting patterns or "patrons" as they were called, were passed down from mother to daughter and the templates were greatly prized by their families. These templates would be built up from simple everyday shapes and objects, such as plates, saucers, leaves and feathers. One quilter even used a hay spade for designing her quilt!

THE TEMPLATES were often made by the quilter's husband, and could be carved from wood, shaped from tin or cut from stiff card. In some cases, cups, glasses and other such objects would be used freely. In later days, templates in celluloid could be purchased. Every generation added their own favourite patterns, and no quilt was the same.

The stitching had the essential function of holding together, the three layers of material, so that when the quilt was washed, the wadding would still be held evenly in place. The stitches also formed the decorative design, creating the three dimensional effect, which gave the quilt its distinctive character.

Selecting and assembling patterns for the design, and then marking them onto the quilt top, was a skilled trade. Usually the whole of the quilt top would be marked out, before the quilt was put into the frames. This was especially necessary for a wholecloth quilt, which was designed around a central pattern, though a strippy quilt could be marked strip by strip when it was in the frame.

Having decided on the design, the patterns would be marked onto the material using a cobbler's awl or sharp needle, to draw around the templates, giving a clear line, which the stitching would follow. When the work was finished, the marking must be removable or be invisible.

The Allendale stampers' quilts were marked out with a blue pencil, which was instantly recognisable. The markings had to remain visible for as long as it took the quilt top to be bought and quilted, which might be weeks or years! Amy Emms would use dressmaker's chalk, to draw on the design, as it would rub off easily. Some quilters would mark one quarter of the design on to greaseproof paper. This was then pricked through on to the quilt top, and repeated for the other quarters.

IN NORTH COUNTRY QUILT MAKING, the quilt frame was regarded as an essential, holding the work in place and enabling even stitching to be done. The frame consisted of two long wooden bars and two flat cross pieces, which were adjustable. The long wooden bars had webbing attached and the back of the quilt was stitched to the webbing, with the length rolled onto the furthest bar. Frames had to be large enough to take the width of the quilt, usually about 90 inches. The layer of wadding, in earlier days, was often some fleecy sheep's wool, though later on it was more usual to use cotton wadding, which could be purchased in rolls from the Co-op Store. In cases of necessity an old blanket could also have been used. The wadding and ready marked quilt top would be laid in place and stitched to the nearest bar, whilst tapes tied around the stretchers, and pinned at intervals to the edge of the material, helped to tension the work. Quilting could now begin.

Cotton or linen thread was used, to sew through the three layers of material in an even running stitch. A short needle was the most convenient, as only a few running stitches could be made at once through the stretched material. A quilter would insist that the left hand, held underneath the frame, should feel the prick of the needle, to ensure that it had pierced all three layers of material. The stitching should be no more than 3/4 inch apart, though Club quilts stitching was not so fine as the more stitches, the longer the quilt took to make.

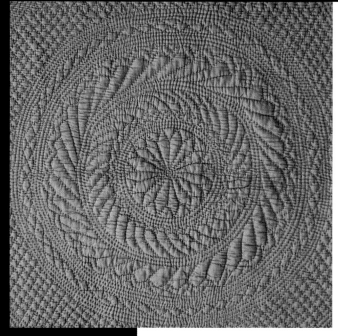

The patterns used in North Country quilts, tended to fall into three types: those used for the central design of the quilt often based around a circular motif, border patterns and patterns for infilling the background.

Central motifs used frequently, were *roses, feather wreaths* and *circles*. A true *lover's knot* was used for a special occasion, and a *wheat sheaf* with *pineapple*, a rather more individual variation.

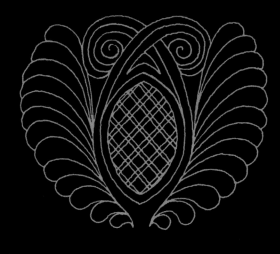

BORDER PATTERNS were used for the outer and inner borders, particularly for wholecloth quilts, but they could also be used for strippy quilts. *Feathers, hammocks* and *cables* were great favourites, and regional variations were developed such as the *Weardale Chain.* A really skilled quilter would ensure that her pattern turned the corners, so that it was unbroken, as a broken border was considered by some to be unlucky!

Amy Emms certainly perfected this technique.

165

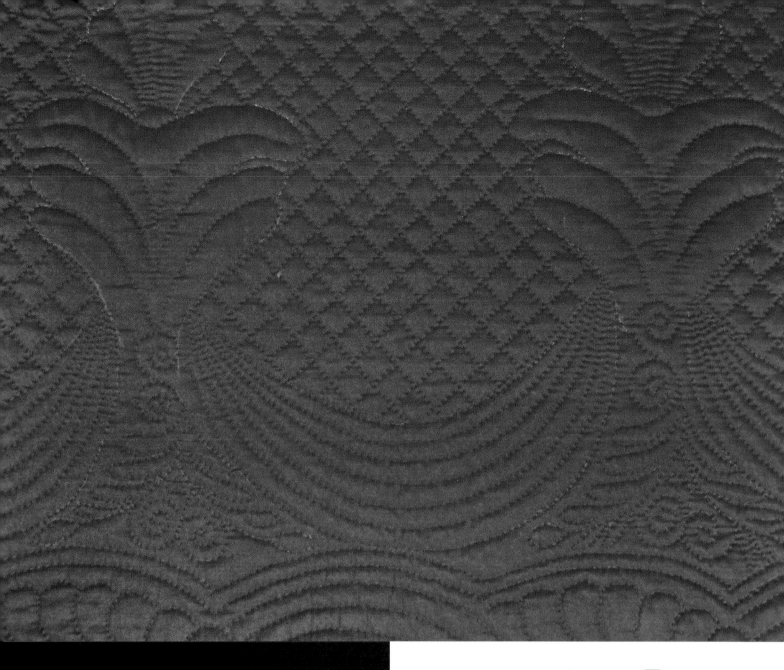

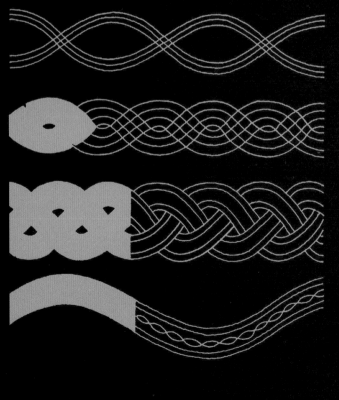

Chain, trail, plait and cable and variations on these patterns, such as worm and bellows are all well used North Country border designs, and have also been used on traditional petticoats.

Prince of Wales' feathers and Fleur de Lis have been incorporated into forms of hammock border patterns and were popular on the stamped Allenheads quilts.

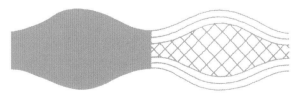

Detail of strippy quilts (top left and right) illustrating trail and rose patterns.
A form of double tulip or bell (bottom) has been used on the border of this petticoat.

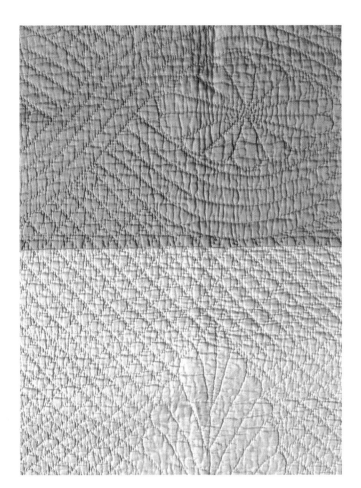
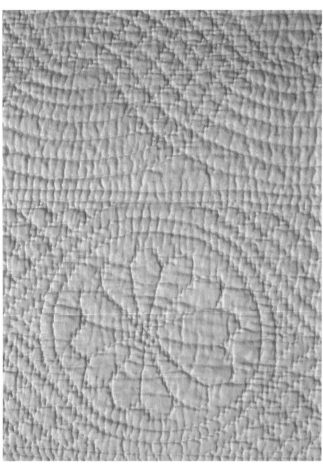

Some designs were specially adapted for use as CORNER PATTERNS, which enabled the quilter to get round the corner without too many complications. Here a *fan* has been used *(inset)* and below the large *shell* design was taken from the seat of a bent wood chair.

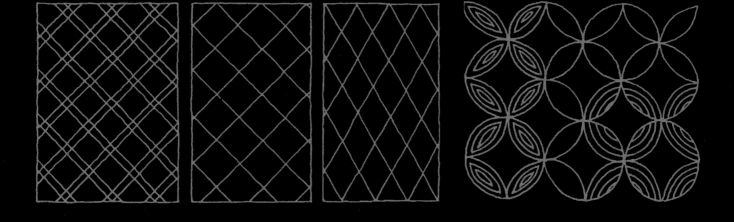

INFILL PATTERNS fill the background areas, between the central motif and the border designs. The most common infill is the *diamond* pattern, which could be *double diamond, square diamond,* and *lozenge diamond.* In Cumberland the *wave* or *zigzag* pattern was well used, where the emphasis was far more on the patchwork rather than on the quilting stitches. Another infill design was *wine glass.*

Great skill was required in marking and stitching the *diamond* infill background. The professionally drawn Allenheads quilts are excellent examples of quilts marked out with great precision.

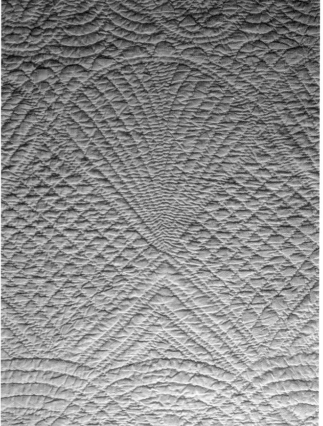

FABRICS AND DYES

D. THOMSON & SONS,
WOOLLEN MANUFACTURERS,
ACKLINGTON PARK, NORTHUMBERLAND.

Traditionally, silk, cotton, linen, and wool, have all been used in the making of quilts and coverlets, in the North of England. The early inventories of the 15th, 16th, and 17th centuries are disappointingly vague about their household's many quilts, though their very listing, would indicate that the quilts and coverlets were much prized, being made of expensive fabrics, such as silks, sarsenets and satins.

WILLIAM JENESON, a Newcastle merchant possessed a 'twilte' worth 6s 8d among his considerable household embroideries in 1587, while in his chest were silk fringes, sewing silk, stitching silk, belmont lace and *'fine sewing skeane threid'*, to the then considerable total of £5.0.0.

Fustian (linen warp and cotton weft), linens and wool were also used, as they were more hardwearing for everyday use. Darlington, in County Durham, had been a noted woollen town in the 13th and 14th centuries, though by the end of the 15th century, wool was being replaced by linen. By the 1590s, there were many linen looms in Darlington, one of the specialities being *"chalon"*, a rough but strong fabric, much used for bedcovers. People at work included silk weavers, chalon weavers, fullers and jersey combers.

The East India Company had begun to import fine Indian cottons and chintzes after 1600. Celia Fiennes, on her travels through Britain, in the late 17th century, noted fine *"Indian quilting"*, Indian being a term for anything exotic or eastern. Their designs and dyes were inevitably imitated throughout Britain.

The North East region and in particular Darlington, had a significant textile trade at the end of the 18th century. By the late 1820s, there were nine linen, and seven worsted mills in the town. Barnard Castle had four mills for spinning wool and Durham had three linen mills and four woollen mills.

In Northumberland there were textile works at Alnwick, Mitford, Berwick, Corbridge, Haltwhistle, Hexham and Morpeth. At Acklington Park, an old iron works was converted in 1791, into a blanket mill, which operated until 1930.

Many of the smaller mills would take in wool fleeces, from local farmers, which were then carded, spun and woven into blankets, cloth or knitting yarn, whatever woollen goods were required. The work was converted to yarn in the mill and sent to local handloom weavers, who produced the blankets and cloth. The woven product was returned to the mill, to be washed and finished ready for use. At Otterburn, on a site believed to go back to the 14th century, the main mill was expanded in 1821, by William Waddell of Jedburgh. Otterburn became well known for providing a service for weaving and finishing cloth for its customers. The mill continued to produce cloth well into the 20th century, and developed a branch at Warwick Bridge near Carlisle.

A number of wholecloth homespun woollen quilts survive in museum collections as well as in the country areas of Northumberland, where they were made. Tullie House Museum, in Carlisle, has a homespun quilt, attributed to Joseph Hedley (Joe the Quilter 1750-1826). The quilt is made of yellow homespun wool with a reverse in light brown wool. Most of these homespun quilts are of wholecloth and are quilted in strips.

Otterburn Mill.

Other woollen quilts, as previously recorded, were made from the "fents" and sample pieces from the mills in Northumberland and on the Borders. Most woollen quilts and coverlets were made for basic utilitarian reasons and provided warmth. Examples of pieced woollen quilts do survive but they tend to be in the minority. A number of quilts were made by tailors, who had an ample supply of left over scraps, from the making of suits, and who also carried sample pieces from the "Scottish Drapers" and the border mills.

Detail quilt ref 2001-10

Detail quilt ref 2001-10

From 1780 up until about 1830, printed cottons had become extremely fashionable in the dress of the period, and were regarded as prestigious materials. These newly popular cotton prints were coming into their own, as printing techniques improved and the range of colours was expanded. Roller printing was gradually replacing block printing, though both printing methods continued alongside each other for many years. Dress prints as well as furnishing fabrics were used for quilts. Prints were often bold and in deep rich colours with a black outline with green being achieved by over dying yellow on blue.

Commemorative medallions were block printed as centrepieces for quilts, and were used for other domestic furnishings, such as cushions and chair backs. They were mass-produced, illustrating chinoiserie themes, so fashionable at this period, as well as floral motifs, baskets and bouquets of flowers. They record events of national importance, such as the wedding of Princess Charlotte of Wales to Prince Leopold of Saxe-Coburg in 1816.

Detail quilt ref 1989-395

Detail quilt ref 1972-658.120

Detail quilt ref 1991-148

Detail quilt ref 1984-150

Detail quilt ref 1990-282

Detail quilt ref 1984-150

Detail quilt ref 1991-148

Shawl motifs and small designs of spots and stripes were much used at this time.

Geometric patterns set within stripes such as the small Maltese cross roller printed pattern, is typical of the 1820s period as is the striped stylised leaf and feather pattern. Woven braid was used to bind the edges of some quilts.

In the North East of England, a directory of 1793, recorded the building of a large cotton mill, on the outskirts of Castle Eden in County Durham, however by 1828, records show that it had fallen into decay. The decline of the textile industry in the North East may have been due in part to the existence of more successful ventures. The development of railways meant that "Manchester goods" could be transported quickly and easily around the country, and the Lancashire mills, more technically advanced, were to become the centre of the cotton printing industry.

Detail quilt ref 1991-148

1830~1860

Due to significant improvements in printing and dyeing techniques, cotton cloth became much cheaper becoming available to the everyday populace. It lost its prestigious status as silks and satins became de rigeur for fashionable dress, thus releasing a large selection of fabrics for quilting. During this period the first practical sewing machine was introduced, speeding up the process of seaming strips of material. The Great Exhibition of 1851 had a huge impact on design styles, helping to enhance the popularity of everything Victorian. Queen Victoria's love affair with Scotland led to tartan cloth becoming fashionable in dress and furnishing fabrics.

From 1840 onwards, American patchwork and appliqué took off, and elaborate pieced arrangements and intricate stitched designs, had an impact on both sides of the Atlantic. The naming of patterns, often relating to the social background of the pioneers, became an important factor, later promulgated by many of the quilting and patchwork magazines. These designs had a significant influence on quilting and patchwork in Britain.

Many earlier designs had come back into favour having been reworked, such as the rainbowing effect, an 1840s repeat of an earlier 1820s pattern.

Top left, detail quilt ref 2006-206   *Above, detail quilt ref 2006-4.2*   *Centre, detail quilt ref 1977-1262*

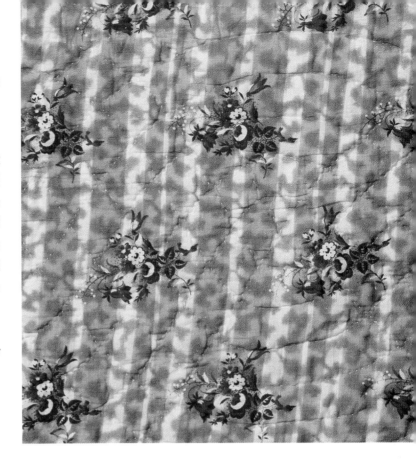

Detail quilt ref 1972-138.2

Carlisle, in Cumberland, became an important textile centre. Ferguson Brothers printed checked and striped cottons from 1837, and Peter Dixon & Sons became one of the largest cotton spinners and manufacturers, employing some 1300 workers in 1836. Stead McAlpin, produced high quality wood block printed textiles at its Cummersdale mill, from 1835.

Striped fabrics with floral motifs were used typically on a blotchy background.

1860 ~ 1880

The vast mass production of cotton textiles meant that there was a noticeable deterioration in design skills. The death of Prince Albert in 1861, threw the nation and Queen Victoria into mourning. Purple often used in two tones or with black was the order of the day. Other drab colours imitating watered silks were introduced. Ultramarine blue came in after 1859 and the crescent moon pattern is typical of the 1870 period.

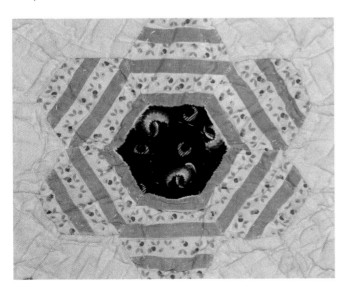

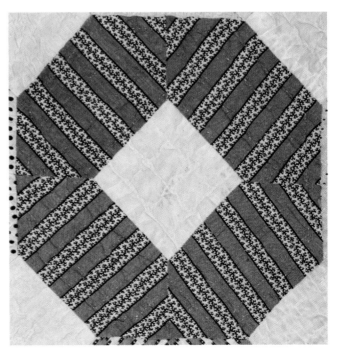

Detail quilt ref 1979-795

Detail quilt ref 1975-265

177

1880~1920

Dress fabrics in cotton were not at all fashionable and tended to be used only by ordinary folk. The cloth had become of poor quality and printed designs were less innovative as many were repeated time and again.

Furnishing fabrics were available and were used in quilts of the period. In 1893, Stead McAlpin acquired the entire works of Bannister Hall, in Preston. This included watercolour designs, wood blocks and pattern books from their works, which had printed fabrics from 1799. Stead McAlpin supplied printed cotton fabrics for quilt makers, and these can be identified and dated from the superb archives, which are still held at Cummersdale, near Carlisle, Cumberland. The ribbon and iris print was a furnishing fabric designed in 1895.

Many Art Nouveau designs were in use and the Arts and Crafts Movement had a distinct impact on the design of these fabrics. A cot coverlet of c. 1900-1905 is made from manufacturer's sample pieces and is typical of the patterns being produced during the period, including one possible fabric by Voysey, of a peacock design in silk.

Centre, detail quilt ref 2004-212
Above, detail of coverlet 1967-176

Until the mid 19th century, all dyestuffs were derived from natural sources. Much research had been carried out into the study and use of dyes and mordants, and their application to different types of cloth. One of the first successfully manufactured dyes, was developed in 1856, by William Henry Perkin, and this was produced commercially in 1857. A gradual transition took place during the 19th century from the use of natural vegetable dyes to dyeing with chemicals. Natural dyes continued to be used, as some of the dyes were still faster than the new synthetic ones.

Dyers notebooks, in the Beamish collections, which belonged to Thomas Ashton of Abbey Mills, Morpeth, who with his brother operated the mill from 1834, give a fascinating insight into the recipes used for dyeing, in the mid 19th century. Notably a recipe for 'Turkey Red on Cotton' appears in the book.

Turkey red became the name given to fabric or yarn, usually cotton, which had been dyed using the Turkey red process. The dye had originated in the East, and had been known by dyers throughout Europe for a number of years, but it was not until the mid 18th century, that it came to Britain from France.

The manufacture of Turkey red was established in Britain in 1785, but was further developed in the mills of South Scotland. A Frenchman, Pierre Jacques Papillon brought the dye over to Glasgow and George Macintosh together with David Dale, who had established the mills at New Lanark with Robert Owen, introduced Turkey red to Scotland, rapidly expanding the cotton printing industry.

The process was quite complicated, involving several washings and steepings of the fabric, in an emulsion prepared from oil, potash and water to which dung had been added. The fabric would be soaked in a weaker solution, without dung, and then washed in a solution of crushed galls. Before the actual dyeing, the cloth was mordanted in alum, and then it could be dyed with madder. After dyeing, the cloth had to be cleared by boiling in olive oil soap and lastly it was brightened in dissolved tin. The result was a fast, bright fabric, which could be used, either as a plain solid colour or overprinted with a "Paisley" design.

Turkey red became commonplace in 19th century quilts and coverlets and they were made throughout Scotland, the North of England, Northern Ireland as well as in the Isle of Man. The red fabric was particularly effective when used with white cotton for strippy quilts, which had appeared in the latter 19th century.

Also combined with green and orange, these solid, bold and fast colours introduced a new vitality to the British quilting scene.

Traditionally, lambs' wool was used to provide the wadding in quilts. It would take about 2 lbs. for a large quilt, and unless bought ready prepared, it had to be well teased or carded, often washed and any dark grease spots removed. In earlier days lambs' wool was preferred as it was light in weight, warmer for use and soft to sew. An alternative was an old blanket or even an old quilt! A W.I. leaflet on quilting issued in 1949 states that *'cotton wool is not advised'*.

Cotton wool was available and was produced in the Manchester mills between 1820 and 1830, and from the mid 19th century was generally replacing wool as the most used filler, except for luxury quilts where lambs' wool was still preferred. Cotton wool was sold in lb packets, as was cotton wadding on a sized backing making it easier to handle. A single layer of cotton wool or wadding was considered adequate for most quilts. Domette, a manufactured woollen lining, which was sold by the yard, was also used. Many of these materials could be purchased from the local Co-op store.

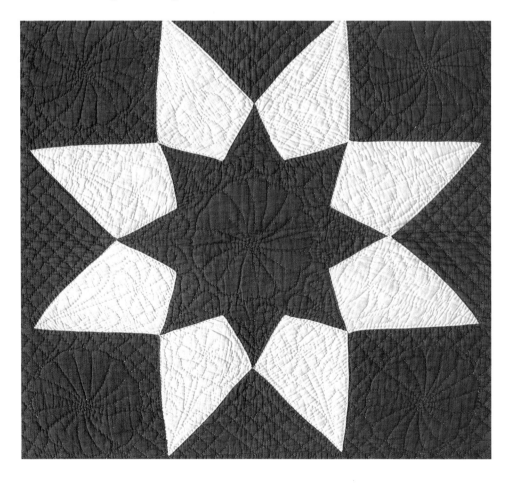

LOOKING AFTER QUILTS

ooking after old quilts at home can be quite challenging, but is usually down to common sense and good housekeeping. First consider where you will store your quilt, and what will affect its long term 'health'. You need to take into account factors such as temperature, humidity, light and general wear and tear, especially if you have pets! If you are at all anxious about your quilt, the best advice is to consult a professional textile conservator. Your local museum should be able to help you find a reliable one in your area.

Cleaning

Wherever possible, try to keep your quilt free of dust. If it is on a bed, ensure that it is covered with a sheet. Dust and dirt cause the fibres to weaken and eventually decay. A vacuum cleaner can be used very gently to remove loose surface dust. It's a good idea to cover the end with some muslin, so that the quilt is not drawn into the cleaner. Do check regularly for moth.

Many quilts will have been well washed during their lifetime, however washing does cause stress and strain to the fabric, and the general rule must be, "if in doubt don't." If you do decide to go ahead and wash your quilt, it is essential to do a test for colour fastness first, and always wash by hand in a large bath, supporting the quilt on another fabric, to carry the weight of the quilt when wet. Never use detergent, or biological powders. Always use a mild soap in lukewarm water. Rinse and allow to drain for several hours before removing to dry flat on a clean sheet in the open air, also covered with another sheet.

Old quilts should never be washed by machine, as there is a danger of stitches being broken, nor should they be dry-cleaned.

Storage

If storing a quilt on a spare bed, ensure that the room is kept at a constant temperature, to prevent damp. The quilt should also be covered, to protect against sunlight, which will rapidly cause it to fade doing irreparable damage.

At Beamish, quilts are stored on large cardboard tubes, (4 ins) diameter, and have a width wider than the quilt. Each tube is covered in aluminium foil and acid free tissue paper, to prevent any acidity from escaping. The quilt, interleaved with acid free tissue paper is carefully rolled onto the tube, ensuring that there are no creases. The tube is then wrapped securely in Tyvek, using a broad cotton tape. Tyvek is a wonderful conservation material, which is waterproof but also allows the quilt to breath. Don't forget to tie a label with a photograph of the quilt onto the outside of the tube!

If you must fold a quilt, to store in a box, first of all, line the box with acid free tissue paper, then using lots more tissue paper, place plenty of rolls of paper along the folds of the quilt to prevent creasing, in order not to weaken the fibres.

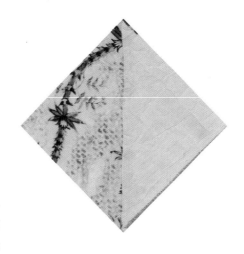

Conservation

Worn quilts are very difficult to clean, without damaging the fabric. Often particular dyes on early quilts have rotted the fabric and may well need extra support. It is sometimes possible to stitch some netting over the damaged area, however it is always better to seek professional advice. Many old pieces of patchwork still retain their original paper patterns, which, should be preserved as part of the quilt's history, and often tell us so much more about an individual piece. Silks, satins and taffetas are definitely the preserve of the professional.

Display

Quilts are there to be enjoyed and it is a pity when they are always hidden away from sight, however they should not be displayed for long periods of time, as when subjected to light, they will eventually fade. They should always be kept away from direct sunlight, and light levels kept to a reasonable level. To hang a quilt, using unbleached calico to make a complete tube about 3 ins wide. Hand stitch the tube or sleeve to the back of the quilt, making sure that the stitches cannot be seen on the right side. Insert a rod or pole and support at each end.

Loops, tacks or pins should never be used as they damage the fabric.

Recording Quilts

Wouldn't it be wonderful if every old quilt had the name of the maker and the date sewn onto it! It is so important to try and find out as much as possible about the history of each quilt, who made it, where and when was it made, also for whom and for what occasion if any. Write the details down, if you know them, on a piece of unbleached fabric, using a waterproof marker pen with a fine point and carefully hand stitch this to the reverse. There may also be interesting stories attached to the quilt about the maker and his or her life that should also be recorded. Our quilts will then live on for future generations to enjoy.

Catalogue of collection

WHOLECLOTH QUILTS

1. Granny Saddler's quilt
Cream cotton sateen on both sides.
Quilting consists of large central rose
surrounded by fourteen smaller roses.
Outer border of running diamond.
Diamond infill.
c. 1935
Willington, Co. Durham
229 x 183 (90 x 72)
Donated by Mrs Powney
Acc.no.1961-77c

2. Allenheads quilt
Cream cotton sateen on both sides.
Quilting design 'stamped' in Allenheads in
1903. Elaborate central design of leaves
and roses. Border of Prince of Wales
feathers with freely drawn corner designs.
Quilted by Mrs. Adamson of Rookhope in
1921. Pencil markings visible.
1903 and 1921
Allenheads, Northumberland and
Rookhope, Co.Durham
274 x 214 (107 x 84)
Donated by Mrs Philipson
Acc.no.1963-58

3. Mrs Fletcher's quilt
Duck egg blue cotton poplin with reverse
of pink cotton poplin. Central quilting
design of two large pineapples with sheaf
between. Outer border of pineapples.
Inner border of half roses and diamond
infill.
1958
Ireshopeburn, Co. Durham
229 x 170 (90 x 67)
Donated by Mrs Fletcher
Acc.no.1963-59

4. Swaledale quilt
Pale blue cotton with reverse of pink
cotton. Very loosely quilted in trail pattern.
Early 1900s
Fremington, N. Yorks
216 x 209 (85 x 82)
Acquired from farm sale
Acc.no.1964-44

5. Barnard Castle quilt
Scarlet cotton with reverse of cream
cotton. Quilting pattern of central rose
with feathers radiating from it. Outer
border of plait with corner rose and
leaf. Diamond infill.
c.1900
Barnard Castle, Co. Durham
229 x 224 (90 x 80)
Donated by Miss F.M.Storey
Acc.no.1967-920.3

6. Butterfly quilt
Plain cotton 'eau de nil' on both sides.
Quilting design of central butterfly in large
circle, surrounded by shells. Outer
butterfly border. Diamond infill.
c.1900
Gainford, Co. Durham
208 x188 (82 x 74)
Donated by Mrs N. Garrick
Acc.no.1969-76

7. South Shields quilt
Pink cotton on both sides though originally
white. Unusual quilted design of lozenge
divided into four with plaits and scale
patterns, all set in large circle. Outer
tulip/bell border. Inner diamond border.
Wineglass infill. The quilt has been
shortened on each side.
c.1850
South Shields, Co. Durham
267 x 203 (105 x 80)
Acc.no.1969-227.37
Donated by Miss E. Kirby

8. Star quilt
Red paisley cotton with reverse of pink
cotton sateen. Quilted with central eight-
pointed star. Outer border of leaves in
groups of four. Inner border of bellows.
Uneven diamond infill.
c. 1920s
Spennymoor, Co. Durham
226 x 200 (89 x 79)
Donated by Mrs G. Lewis
Acc.no.1970-228

9. Quebec quilt
Pale blue cotton with pale pink cotton
reverse. Quilting in Allenheads style with
central rose, with leaves and roses
radiating from the centre. Outer border of
hammock and lily.
c.1900
Quebec, Co.Durham
216 x 214 (85 x 84)
Donated by Mrs M. Ridley
Acc.no.1970-497

10. Plain quilt
Blue, beige and pink printed cotton with
reverse of white cotton. Very loosely
quilted overall in trail
c.1900
Provenance not known
229 x 208 (1971-16.4)
Anonymous donation
Acc.no.1971-16.4

11. Plain white quilt
White cotton sateen on both sides.
Quilting in strips of worm enclosing shell
and running diamond and rose.
c.1920
Provenance not known
264 x 244 (104 x 96)
Anonymous donation
Acc.no.1971-16.9

12. Plain white quilt
White cotton sateen on both sides. Quilted
with large central rose and fourteen
smaller roses. Quilting in strips of trail,
diamond and overlapping fan.
c.1900
Provenance not known
249 x 217 (98 x 85)
Acc.no.1976-16.10

13. Plain gold quilt
Mustard/gold cotton sateen with pink and
gold floral printed cotton reverse. Quilted
with small central star enclosed by feather
circle and eight roses. Outer border of
twist. Inner border of chain enclosing rose.
Diamond infill.
c. 1910
Crook, Co. Durham
224 x 196 (88 x 77)
Donated by Mrs Burdett
Acc. no.1971-241

14. Plain green quilt
Green cotton sateen with pink cotton
sateen reverse. Quilting consists of large
central whorl in feather circle. Outer
border of double running feather. Diamond
infill. Made by Mrs.Lowe of Spennymoor,
and traditional family design.
c.1940
Spennymoor, Co. Durham
228 x 204 (90 x 80)
Donated by Mrs A.Lowe
Acc.no.1971-264

15. Plain white quilt
White cotton on both sides. Quilting is in
strips of twist, worm enclosing rose,
running diamond enclosing rose repeated.
Donated by the Misses Armstrong
Acc.no.1971-335.67

16. Hayspade quilt
White cotton on both sides, quilted overall
in hayspade pattern. The quilter Mrs A.
Ireland used a hayspade as template.
Diamond infill.
1920
Thornaby, N.Yorks
234 x 211 (92 x 83)
Donated by Mrs A. Ireland
Acc.no.1972-4

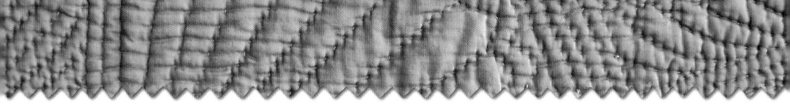

17. Plain white quilt
White cotton on both sides. Very finely quilted with large central circle enclosing stylised leaf pattern. Outer border on three sides only of eleven large circles, enclosing stylised leaf pattern.
c.1860
Northumberland
246 x 239 (97 x 94)
Donated by Miss Winifred Smith
Acc.no.1972-52

18. Plain floral quilt
Pale printed floral cotton with reverse of scarlet and cream floral cotton. Quilting in strips of twist, bellows and running diamond. Made by Mrs Harriet King (born 1866 in Suffolk) who moved to Quebec in 1886, with her husband who was looking for work in the mines.
1886
Quebec, Co. Durham
251 x 224 (99 x 88)
Donated by Mrs Audrey Cox
Acc.no.1972-358

19. Plain gold quilt
Gold cotton sateen on both sides. Very finely quilted with central rose enclosed by circle, with elaborate design of leaves, flowers and feathers radiating from the centre. Made by Mrs Mary Potts, a widow and well-known quilter, who made her living by quilting in Chester le Street.
1939
Chester le Street, Co. Durham
234 x 213 (92 x 84)
Donated by Mrs Jobling
Acc.no.1972-555

20. Allenheads quilt
Cream cotton sateen on both sides. Very fine quilting with central rose and elaborate design of leaves, feathers and roses radiating from the centre. Outer border of hammock and rose. Quilting is in the Allenheads style.
c.1900
Haydon Bridge, Northumberland
274 x 246 (108 x 97)
Donated by Mr D.F.Wadge
Acc.no.1972-658.118

21. Gold homespun quilt
Homespun gold woollen material on both sides. No central design. Outer border of broken chains, enclosing stylised flower. Inner border of running diamond. Centre with diamond infill.
c.1860
Haydon Bridge, Northumberland
234 x 196 (92 x 77)
Donated by Mr D.F.Wadge
Acc.no.1972-658.124

22. Allenheads quilt
White cotton sateen on both sides. Quilting consists of central ring enclosing rose with freely drawn leaves and roses radiating from the centre. Outer border of curled feathers and roses and elaborate corner design. Blue 'stamped' pencil markings visible typical of Allenheads work.
c.1900
Haydon Bridge, Northumberland
255 x 227 (100 x 89)
Donated by Mr D.F.Wadge
Acc.no.1972-658.129

23. Plain white quilt
Cream sateen cotton with reverse of blue printed cotton. Very simple quilted design of plain diamonds. Wineglass border with large fans at inner corners. Made by Mrs Jane Robson of Benwell.
1935
Benwell, Newcastle upon Tyne
224 x 211 (88 x 83)
Donated by Mrs E.M. Cameron
Acc.no.1976-125.1

24. Plain floral quilt
Pink, yellow and white flowered cotton print with reverse of white cotton. Quilting design consists of large circle with feathers and roses radiating from it. Outer fan border and corner design. Made by Mrs Alice Pow of North Shields for her trousseau. She was married aged 27 years old in 1888.
c.1888
North Shields, Northumberland
218 x 201 (86 x 79)
Donated by Mrs R. Pow
Acc.no.1976-310.2

25. Club quilt
Ivory cotton sateen on both sides. Quilting design consists of central rose with leaves and roses radiating from the centre. Outer border of hammock. Diamond infill. Quilt design may have been influenced by Allenheads style. Made by Mrs Ellen Robson, a miner's widow who brought up her family of nine children by her income from quilting.
1910-1920
Ryhope, Co. Durham
231 x 213 (91 x 84)
Donated by Mrs M.L.Johnson
Acc.no.1976-656

26. Plain white quilt
White cotton sateen on both sides. Quilting consists of twelve running feathers along the length of the quilt arranged in pairs to form a bellows pattern. Diamond infill.
c.1880
Low Fell, Co. Durham
234 x 221 (92 x 87)
Donated by Mrs M.E.Taylor
Acc.no.1976-847.1

27. Plain pink quilt
Very pale pink cotton on both sides. Quilting in the Allenheads style of central rose and radiating feathers, leaves and roses. Outer border of hammock with diamond infill. The quilt has been reduced in size.
c. 1900
Provenance not known
196 x 124 (77 x 49)
Anonymous donation
Acc.no.1977-1239

28. Plain green quilt
Green cotton sateen with reverse of pink cotton sateen. Quilting design of central flower in feather circle. Outer border of roses with fans in each corner. Inner border of running feather. Frill around three edges.
c.1900
Neville's Cross, Durham
261 x 258 (103 x 102)
Donated by Mrs Lee
Acc.no.1978-946

29. Plain floral quilt
Cream cotton, printed with small clusters of flowers in gold and red. Reverse of cream cotton. Quilted in strips of bellows enclosing plait, fan and bellows.
c. 1890
Byker, Newcastle upon Tyne
236 x 203 (93 x 80)
Donated by Mrs Finlay
Acc.no.1978-1191.7

30. Old Joe's quilt
White cotton on both sides. Very finely quilted with central star enclosed in circle. Outer twist border, inner zigzag and fan border. Diamond infill. Only two thirds of this quilt survives. The quilt was ordered and bought direct from Joe the Quilter by the English family who owned Humshaugh Mill.
c. 1820
Humshaugh, Northumberland
251 x 165 (99 x 65)
Donated by Mr J A Herdman
Acc.no.1979-442

31. Club Quilt
Cream cotton sateen on both sides, quilted with large central chain circle enclosing eight leaves. Outer border of plait and inner border of running feather, diamond infill. The quilt was made by Mrs Bond, a miner's widow of Hetton le Hole.
c. 1910
Hetton le Hole, Co. Durham
224 x 198 (88 x 78)
Donated by Mr J S Wade
Acc.no.1979-452

32. Church club quilt

Very pale pink cotton sateen with reverse
of very pale lemon sateen. Central rose
with leaves, roses and feathers radiating
from centre. Corner swags, outer border of
stylised leaf pattern. Diamond infill.
1907
Percy Main, Northumberland
251 x 236 (99 x 93)
Donated by Mrs V Mills
Acc.no.1979-837

33. Plain Quilt

Pale pink cotton with reverse of printed
roses in red and black cotton. The quilt is
not complete. Centre quilted with large
lover's knot. Border of running feather.
Diamond infill.
c.1910
Not known
168 x 155 (66 x 61)
Anonymous donation
Acc.no.1979-916

34. Plain red spotted quilt

Red cotton with overall cream spots and
reverse of red paisley printed cotton.
Another older quilt appears to be acting as
padding for this one. Very loosely quilted
overall.
c. 1890
Not known
216 x 185 (85 x 73)
Anonymous donation
Acc.no.1979-918

35. Plain green quilt

Pale green cotton sateen on both sides
with strip of cream and red floral printed
material along two outer edges to
strengthen. Quilted with large central
diamond/square, feather pattern, and outer
running diamond.
c. 1910
Not known
211 x 183 (83 x 72)
Anonymous donation
Acc.no.1979-919

36. Simonside quilt

Gold cotton sateen with reverse of printed
floral cotton. Quilted in strips of twist and
running diamond alternately. Made by
Mrs Helen Laidler for her daughter's
"bottom drawer". Margaret Laidler
married in 1904.
Simonside, South Shields, Co. Durham
249 x 234 (98 x 92)
Donated by Miss N Hutchinson
Acc.no.1980-500

37. Mrs Shepherd's quilt

Peach cotton sateen with reverse of yellow
sateen. Quilted with central rose and four
flowers in circular twist. Outer border of
large shells. Diamond infill. Made by Mrs
M E Shepherd of Amble [brought up on
Coquet Island] who ran quilting clubs to
help support her family after her husband
was injured in the pit.
c. 1935
Amble, Northumberland
254 x 214 (100 x 84)
Donated by Miss B Shepherd
Acc.no.1980-744

38. Plain pink quilt

Peach/pink cotton sateen with cream
cotton sateen reverse. Quilted with central
rose and a rose in each corner, also twelve
other simple roses equally spaced around
the quilt. Diamond infill and leaves.
Outer feather border.
c. 1920
218 x 196 (86 x 77)
Donated by Mr H Nye
Acc.no.1980-780

39. Plain beige quilt

Golden beige cotton sateen on both sides,
quilted with large central rose in feather
circle, outer feather wreath border.
Diamond infill. Frill all round. Bought
originally from a quilting club in the West
Rainton area.
c. 1910
West Rainton, Co Durham
251 x 246 (99 x 97)
Donated by Mrs R Turner
Acc.no.1980-862

40. Homespun quilt

Saffron hand spun and woven woollen
quilt with beige reverse. Quilted in large
fan shapes with diamond infill.
c. 1860
Greenhead, Northumberland
218 x 163 (86 x 64)
Acquired
Acc.no.1980-884.2

41. Plain cream quilt

Cream cotton with small printed mauve
flowers on both sides. Quilted overall in
flower pattern – four petalled stylised.
c. 1920
Seaburn, Co Durham
229 x 224 (90 x 88)
Donated by Mrs Thompson
Acc.no.1981-214

42. Plain lemon quilt

Lemon cotton sateen with reverse of white
cotton sateen. Quilted in strips of twist,
large chain with flower, plait, running
diamond with flower and running feather.
c. 1920
Darlington, Co. Durham
244 x 218 (96 x 86)
Donated by Mrs M E Forster
Acc.no.1981-225

43. Club quilt

Pale gold cotton sateen on both sides.
Quilting design of central rose with leaves,
feathers and flowers radiating from centre.
Outer border of elaborate freely drawn
design. Diamond infill. Whole quilt would
seem to have been influenced by
Allenheads style. This quilt was made by a
club in aid of Alston Town Hall funds.
c. 1930
Alston, Cumberland
256 x 229 (101 x 90)
Donated by Mr & Mrs Ben Dickinson
Acc.no.1982-27

44. Plain quilt

Blue cotton sateen on both sides. Quilted
with large centre design composed of
stylised leaves surrounded by a feather
circle. Outer border of bellows. Diamond
infill.
c. 1930
Page Bank, Co. Durham
216 x 188 (85 x 74)
Anonymous donation
Acc.no.1983-266.12

45. Plain quilt

Very pale peach pink cotton sateen with
reverse of cream cotton sateen, quilted
with large central rose with feather circle.
Outer border of twist with a star in each
corner. Inner border of alternate cross and
circle. Inmost border of trail, shell or
mother of thousands infill. Made by a
Pelton lady.
c. 1914
Pelton, Co Durham
236 x 216 (93 x 85)
Donated by Mrs Steel
Acc.no.1984-63.1

46. Plain quilt

Lemon cotton sateen with reverse of pale
lemon cotton sateen. Quilted with design
of twelve squares enclosing flower, outer
border of feather swags. Overall infill.
Quilt made by Mrs Carr of Lumley.
c. 1920
Lumley, Co. Durham
239 x 211 (94 x 83)
Donated by Mrs Steel
Acc.no.1984-63.2

47. Plain quilt

Peach cotton sateen with reverse of very
pale green cotton sateen. Quilting design
similar to Cat.no.45.
c. 1920
Lumley, Co. Durham
226 x 190 (89 x 74)
Donated by Mrs Steel
Acc.no.1984-63

48. Plain white quilt
White cotton sateen on both sides. Quilting of central rose with stylised leaves, flowers and feathers radiating from centre. Outer border of running feather with rose in each corner. Diamond infill. In style of Allenheads quilts.
c. 1890
Not known
218 x 163 (86 x 64)
Anonymous donation
Acc.no.1984-71

49. Plain white quilt
White cotton sateen on both sides. Quilted in strips of trail, rose, running diamond with star and running feather.
c. 1900
239 x 193 (94 x 76)
Anonymous donation
Acc.no.1984-72

50. Green & lemon quilt
Quilt of green cotton sateen with reverse of lemon cotton sateen. Central quilted rose enclosed by feather circle. Outer border of twist with roses in each corner. Inner border of diamonds and roses.
c. 1910-20
Consett, Co. Durham
225 x 185 (89 x 73)
Donated by Mr & Mrs Conney
Acc.no.1986-128

51. White wholecloth quilt
White cotton on both sides. Has been reduced in size to single quilt by machine stitching. The quilt is quilted in strips of twist, worm & rose, running feather and wineglass.
c. 1870
Seaham, Co. Durham
196 x 190 (77 x 75)
Donated by Miss F Bryan
Acc.no.1988-117

52. Mary Lough's quilt
Wholecloth quilt in peach crepe de chine. Large central feather circle and outer border of feather hammocks. Diamond infill. The edges are piped and hand stitched.
c. 1950/60
Witton le Wear, Co. Durham
224 x 223 (88 x 88)
Donated by Mrs Burtt
Acc.no.1989-217

53. Mustard wholecloth quilt
Quilt of mustard cotton and reverse of pink cotton. Quilted overall with large central design of feathers, leaves and roses with diamond infill. Outer border of swag and roses. Made by Mrs Elizabeth Grainger.
c. 1900-20
Seaton Sluice, Northumberland
232 x 214 (91 x 84)
Donated by Miss Hannah Grainger
Acc.no.1989-237.19

54. Homespun wholecloth quilt
Homespun red wool top with reverse of khaki homespun wool. Probably hand dyed. The quilting is in strips of trail enclosing leaf, rose in circle, bellows enclosing leaf and diamond enclosing whorl.
c. 1875-1900
Elsdon/Rothbury, Northumberland
224 x 223 (88 x 88)
Acquired
Acc.no.1990-101.3

55. Stamped wholecloth quilt
Quilt of white cotton on both sides. Central rose with leaves and roses radiating from the centre. Outer hammock, fleur de lis border. Diamond infill. Quilt shows signs of blue pencil marking typical of Allenheads, though made by donor's grandmother Mrs Kelly.
c. 1890-1900
Whitley Bay, Northumberland
248 x 218 (98 x86)
Donated by Mr & Mrs Harrison
Acc.no.1991-127

56. Cream wholecloth quilt
Wholecloth quilt of cream cotton sateen on both sides. Central feather circle enclosing rose surrounded by roses and feathers set on background of diamond infill. Outer feather border.
Pre 1929
Eldon, Bishop Auckland, Co. Durham
231 x 197 (91 x 78)
Donated by Mrs Gray
Acc.no.1991-128

57. Stamped wholecloth quilt
Cream cotton sateen on both sides with clearly marked blue pencil design. Quilted with central rose with radiating feathers set in large circle. Outer feather border forming hammocks with roses in each corner. Quilt made by Caroline Swinbanks, a miner's wife, whose husband died of pneumonia when their youngest daughter was only 2 weeks old. Caroline began to run quilt clubs. She made this quilt when about 27 years old as a wedding present for her niece Caroline Dobinson.
1914
Burnopfield, Co. Durham
233 x 207 (92 x 81)
Donated by Mrs Collis
Acc.no.1991-237

58. Cream wholecloth quilt
Cream cotton sateen on both sides. Quilted with central rose in feather circle with leaves and roses radiating from the centre in Allenheads style. Outer hammock, fleur de lis border and diamond infill. Quilt made by Mrs Agnes Johnson of Blyth who made quilts for her family and also for the church. She had been apprenticed to a dressmaker.
1942
Blyth, Northumberland
253 x 211 (100 x 83}
Donated by Mrs Hayes
Acc.no.1992-2

59. Green wholecloth
Green cotton sateen wholecloth with reverse of gold cotton sateen. Quilted with central rose surrounded by eight leaves set on a diamond infill background. Outer feather hammock border with roses in each corner. Made by Frances Teasdale and Emily Logan of South Moor, Stanley.
c. 1930
South Moor, Stanley, Co. Durham
240 x 189 (94 x 74)
Donated by Mrs M Brooks
Acc.no.1992-79.1

60. Turkey red paisley wholecloth quilt
Turkey red cotton with reverse of red paisley cotton. Quilted in strips of twist. Made by Miss Elizabeth Beck from a lead-mining family.
c. 1890-1900
Blanchland, Northumberland
229 x 201 (90 x 79)
Donated by Mrs Urwin
Acc.no.1993-4.2

61. White wholecloth quilt
White cotton sateen on both sides. Quilt in the Allenheads style with central leaves design and outer border of hammock and fleur de lis. Blue pencil markings are visible.
c. 1920
Corbridge, Northumberland
267 x 211 (105 x 83)
Donated by Robert & John Smith in memory of their late mother Mrs Jean Smith.
Acc.no.1993-171

62. Homespun wholecloth quilt
Homespun wholecloth quilt in maroon dyed wool.
The quilt was made by the donor's mother Mrs Katherine Tubridy who was a farmer's wife from County Clare in S. Ireland.
c. 1930
County Clare, S. Ireland
196 x 190 (77 x 75)
Donated by Mrs C Wilcox
Acc.no.1994-119

63. Cream and coffee wholecloth quilt

Cream cotton sateen with coffee cotton sateen reverse. Quilted with large flowing central design of leaves and roses. Outer hammock border and diamond infill. Outer frill. Blue markings on quilt still visible. Made by Mrs Matilda Clish.
c. 1900-20
Annfield Plain, Co. Durham
246 x 223 (97 x 88)
Donated by Miss L. Clish
Acc.no.1994-121.1

64. Wholecloth quilt

Oyster cotton sateen with reverse of printed floral material. Quilted outer border in twist with infill of scallop. Made by Mrs Matilda Clish.
c. 1900-20
Annfield Plain, Co. Durham
217 x 188 (85 x 74)
Donated by Miss L. Clish
Acc.no.1994-121.3

65. Pink wholecloth quilt

Pink cotton sateen with reverse of cream cotton sateen. Quilted with large central circle enclosing rose on a diamond background. Made by donor's grandmother, Margaret Jobson, a nurse at Fever Hospital near Barnard Castle.
c. 1920
Middleton in Teesdale
245 x 205 (96 x 81)
Donated by Mrs. J Purt
Acc.no.1997-79.1

66. White wholecloth quilt

White cotton with reverse of white cotton marked Horrockses. Quilted with central rose surrounded by large circle of radiating leaves and feathers. Unusual outer border of C design with leaves. Blue pencil marking still visible. Made by one of the Davison family – farmers.
c. 1910
Castleside, Co. Durham
241 x 193 (95 x 76)
Donated by Mrs Higgins & Mrs Peart
Acc.no.2001-33

67. White wholecloth quilt

White cotton with reverse of white cotton. Blue pencil markings still visible. Quilted design of eight leaves surrounded by hammock circle. Outer border of four-leaf pattern with true lover's knot in each corner. Diamond infill. Probably made by Mary Jane Turnbull in her early 20s.
Pre. 1906
Leadgate, Co. Durham
267 x 217 (105 x 85)
Donated by Mr.I.Armstrong
Acc.no.2001-41.1

68. Cream wholecloth quilt

Cream cotton sateen with reverse of pale green cotton sateen. Quilted central design of leaves and roses with outer border of roses. Diamond infill. Machined edges.
c. 1900-10
Durham/Northumberland
233 x 194 (92 x 76)
Anonymous donation
Acc.no.2003-172

69. Wholecloth quilt

Tomato cotton sateen with reverse of lemon cotton sateen. The quilting is in strips of running feather with diamond infill. Belonged to Rosanna Laycock. Outer edges machined.
c. 1920-30
Burnhope, Co. Durham
243 x 212 (96 x 83)
Donated by Mr Alan Heslop
Acc.no.2004-141

70. Wholecloth quilt

Yellow cotton sateen with reverse of pink satin rayon. Central design quilted with running feather enclosing three roses. Outer and inner borders of twist. Machine stitched edging.
Made by Mrs Isobel Williams, (1894 - 1954), mother of twelve children and grandmother of donor. This quilt was made for her grandson William Williams when he married. Isobel took orders from and made quilts for Blacketts of Sunderland.
1939
Monkwearmouth, Sunderland
232 x 192 (91 x 76)
Donated by Mrs Liddell
Acc.no.2006-115

71. Wholecloth quilt

Pink cotton sateen with reverse of white cotton sateen. Blue pencil markings are visible on the pink side. Centre of running feather design with corners in stylised leaf pattern. Pattern very similar to 2001-33. Made by Mrs.A.V.Lister, (born 1903).
c. 1920s/30s
Castleside, Co. Durham
246 x 208 (97 x 82)
Donated by Mr. And Mrs. Freak
Acc.no. 2006-167

WHOLECLOTH QUILTS WITH BORDERS

72. Club quilt

White cotton sateen on both sides, upper side has a printed border of floral printed cotton in reds and golds. Quilting in large central circle enclosing eight roses, outer border of twist, inner border of running feather with diamond infill. The quilt was made by Mrs Sally Ranson.
c. 1890
New Seaham, Co. Durham
221 x 203 (87 x 80)
Donated by Mrs M J Smith
Acc.no.1971-306

73. Club quilt

Cream cotton sateen with printed border in gold, blue and green. Reverse of pink cotton sateen with printed border in gold, pink and blue. Quilting of central flower enclosing cross. Outer running feather border, inner hammock border, diamond infill. Made by Mrs Stewart.
c. 1910
Bowburn, Co. Durham
243 x 211 (96 x 83)
Donated by Mrs M Bowman
Acc.no.1971-374

74. Willington quilt

Black cotton sateen with gold cotton sateen border. Reverse of gold sateen with black border. Quilting of central scissor pattern, corner design of stylised leaf. Outer border of worm enclosing chain. Diamond infill.
c. 1890
Willington, Co. Durham
200 x 166 (79 x 65)
Donated by Mr Armstrong
Acc.no.1971-397

75. Bordered quilt

Green cotton sateen with printed floral border of cream, green and red. Deep red strip along each short end. Reverse of deep red cotton sateen. Quilted in strips of worm, bellows, plait, running diamond and central plait.
c. 1880
Not known
206 x 206 (81 x 81)
Anonymous donation
Acc.no.1977-1241

76. Bordered quilt

Mauve cotton sateen with printed border of rose pink and white roses. Reverse of cream cotton sateen. Quilting design of central rose with lines radiating from centre. Leaf pattern inside lined inner border of hammock. Outer border of large chain on printed material.
c. 1880
Not known
229 x 208 (90 x 82)
Anonymous donation
Acc.no.1984-78

STRIPPY QUILTS

77. Swaledale strippy
Pink and white, striped cotton and white cotton strips. Reverse of white cotton, very loosely quilted in trail. The quilting follows the strips.
c. 1900
Grinton, N. Yorks
209 x 204 (82 x 80)
Donated by Mr F E Horn
Acc.no.1961-59b

78. Swaledale strippy
Nine narrow strips of floral printed cotton. Reverse of white cotton. Quilting follows the strips in twist.
c. 1900
Grinton, N. Yorks
216 x 212 (85 x 83)
Donated by Mr F E Horn
Acc.no.1961-59c

79. Swaledale strippy
Printed cotton in five white and four pink strips. Reverse of white cotton. Quilting follows the strips in twist.
c. 1900
Grinton, N. Yorks
214 x 214 (84 x 84)
Donated by Mr F E Horn
Acc.no.1961-59e

80. Patchwork strippy
Printed cottons in pale blue, pink, gold, cream and Turkey red. Reverse of white cotton. Quilt consists of five narrow strips and four broad strips of pieced square. Quilting in twist, rose, running diamond and bellows. Made by Miss Sarah Egglestone.
c. 1890
Westgate, Co. Durham
234 x 188 (92 x 74)
Donated by Miss M Watson
Acc.no.1962-140

81. Leaf strippy
Printed cotton strips, seven printed blue strips and six white strips. Reverse of white cotton. Quilting in single leaf and diamond infill, follow the strips. Made by Mrs Harriet Adamson.
c. 1900
Rookhope, Co. Durham
228 x 228 (90 x 90)
Donated by Mrs Philipson
Acc.no.1962-141

82. Weardale chain strippy
Printed and plain cotton strips, six pink and five blue and white striped strips. Quilting in feather twist, rose, running feather. Weardale chain, running feather Weardale chain, running feather and leaf and feather. Made by Mrs Harriet Walton.
c. 1933
Frosterley, Co. Durham
208 x 194 (82 x 76)
Donated by Mrs M Robinson
Acc.no.1962-142

83. Lover's knot strippy
Turkey red and white cotton strips with reverse of white cotton. The quilting does not follow the strips, central lover's knot. Outer twist border, inner leaf border. Wine glass infill.
c. 1870
West Cornforth, Co. Durham
227 x 173 (89 x 68)
Donated by Mrs Soulsby
Acc.no.1962-143

84. Turkey red and cream strippy
Turkey red and cream cotton with reverse of cream cotton. Six broad red strips, five narrow red strips and ten narrow cream strips. Quilting follows the strips in hammock, double hammock and running diamond.
c. 1883
Wearhead, Co. Durham
222 x 209 (87 x 82)
Donated by Miss M H Graham
Acc.no.1963-57

85. Chintz strippy
Brown, mustard and pink chintzes, one with birds. Reverse of white calico. Nine strips of three types of chintz. Quilting does not follow the strips. Outer border of running diamond, inner border of hammock. Wineglass infill.
c. 1830
Barrasford, Northumberland
269 x 259 (106 x 102)
Donated by Mrs L Straughan
Acc.no.1963-526

86. Swaledale strippy
Pink and white and blue and white printed cotton strips. Reverse of white cotton. Very loosely quilted, following but not coinciding with strips, in trail.
c. 1910
Fremington, N. Yorks
216 x 208 (85 x 82)
Acquired from farm sale
Acc.no.1964-43

87. Pink and white strippy
Plain cottons in deep pink and white, reverse or plain white cotton. Nine strips in all, quilted in fan, double hammock, trail, running feather and single hammock, following the strips.
c. 1880
Newcastle upon Tyne
244 x 217 (96 x 85)
Donated by Mrs Stone
Acc.no.1964-1098

88. Pink and white strippy
Plain cottons in deep pink and white. Reverse of pink cotton, four white and three pink strips. Quilting follows the strips in running feather, rose, worm and twist.
c. 1890
Easington, Co. Durham
230 x 179 (91 x 70)
Donated by Mrs V S Robson
Acc.no.1966-45

89. Pink and cream strippy
Plain cottons in pink and cream. Reverse of cream cotton. Five pink strips and four cream strips. Quilting does not follow the strips. Outer border of leaf, inner border of feather. Diamond infill each corner and across centre of quilt.
c. 1900
Barnard Castle, Co. Durham
244 x 213 (96 x 84)
Donated by Miss F M Storey
Acc.no.1967-920.2

90. Pink and blue strippy
Plain cottons in pink and plain blue. Reverse of white cotton. Seven pink strips and six pale blue strips. Quilting follows the strips in trail and Weardale chain alternately.
c. 1900
Barnard Castle, Co. Durham
252 x 229 (99 x 90)
Donated by Miss F M Storey
Acc.no.1967-920.4

91. Chintz strippy quilt
Printed chintzes. Reverse of red and cream chintz. Five red chintz strips and four cream chintz strips. Quilting follows the strips in fan, worm, double hammock and running feather.
c. 1890
Durham
234 x 219 (92 x 86)
Donated by Misses Gordon
Acc.no.1968-67.1

92. Pink and white strippy
Plain cottons in pink and white. Reverse of white cotton. Five pink and five white strips. Quilting follows the strips in twist and wineglass alternately. Probably made by a miner's wife.
c. 1890
Durham
230 x 193 (91 x 76)
Donated by the Misses Gordon
Acc.no.1968-67.2

93. Chintz strippy
Printed chintzes in cream, brown, pink and mustard. Reverse of cream calico. Thirteen strips in all. Quilting follows the strips in zigzag, small diamonds and twist.
c. 1830/40
Dinnington, Northumberland
254 x 249 (100 x 98)
Donated by Miss B E White
Acc.no.1970-90.7

94. Paisley strippy
Printed red paisley and plain white cotton. Reverse of pink and white cotton, four red and five white strips. Quilting follows the strips in worm, bellows, running diamond, twist and running feather.
c. 1890
Not known
246 x 224 (97 x 88)
Acc.no.1971-16.6

95. Turkey red and white strippy
Red and white cotton. Reverse of white cotton. Five Turkey red and six white strips. Quilting follows the strips in stylised four-leaved flower and two rows of chain alternately. Quilt made by Mrs Jane Kidd.
c. 1890
Rothbury, Northumberland
244 x 221 (96 x 87)
Donated by Miss E Turnbull
Acc.no.1971-175.3

96. Turkey red and white strippy
Red and white cotton. Reverse of white cotton. Five Turkey red and four white strips. Quilting follows the strips in zigzag, twist and chain.
c. 1900
Sunderland, Co. Durham
248 x 234 (98 x 92)
Donated by Mr S A Staddon
Acc.no.1971-388.4

97. Turkey red and white strippy
Red and white cotton. Reverse of white cotton. Six Turkey red and six white strips. Quilting follows the strips in running feather and diamond alternately. Quilt made by a Miss Nixon who ran a quilting club in the Slaley area.
c. 1870-80
Slaley, Northumberland
239 x 216 (94 x 85)
Donated by Mrs Isabel Nixon
Acc.no.1972-97

98. Blue and pink strippy
Plain blue and printed pink cotton. Reverse of white cotton. Four blue and four printed pink stripes. Quilting follows the strips in zigzag, twist and scallop. Made by Mrs Phillipson of Rispby (between Rookhope and Wolfcleugh).
Pre 1855
Rookhope, Co. Durham
257 x 218 (101 x 86)
Donated by Mr A Nunn
Acc.no.1972-138

99. Turkey red and orange strippy
Printed Turkey red and orange cotton. Reverse of beige and brown cotton. Seven red and seven orange strips. Quilting follows the strips in curled leaf, plait, ring and star chain, heart chain and trail.
c. 1870
Haydon Bridge, Northumberland
254 x 249 (100 x 98)
Donated by Mr D F Wadge
Acc.no.1972-658.119

100. Blue and cream strippy
Pale blue and cream printed cotton. Reverse of red and cream cotton. Six blue strips and five cream strips. Quilting follows the strips in wave enclosing chain, ring chain, zigzag, feather and double hammock.
c. 1870
Haydon Bridge, Northumberland
241 x 211 (95 x 83)
Donated by Mr D F Wadge
Acc.no.1972-658.121

101. Pink and white strippy
Printed pink and white cotton. Reverse of white cotton. Seven wide pink strips and six narrower printed floral strips. Quilting follows the strips in scallop, twist and running feather with diamond infill.
c. 1900
Haydon Bridge, Northumberland
259 x 234 (102 x 92)
Donated by Mr D F Wadge
Acc.no.1972-658.122

102. Green and white strippy
Green and white calico. Reverse of white calico. Five white and four green strips. Quilting follows the strips in plait and double tulip alternatively.
c. 1870
Haydon Bridge, Northumberland
254 x 226 (100 x 89)
Donated by Mr D F Wadge
Acc.no.1972-658.12

103. Floral strippy
Floral printed cotton. Reverse of white cotton, five strips of dark printed material and four strips of white material. Quilting follows the strips in double hammock and running feather. Diamond infill.
c. 1870
Haydon Bridge, Northumberland
254 x 211 (100 x 83)
Donated by Mr D F Wadge
Acc.no.1972-658.125

104. Turkey red and white strippy
Turkey red twill and white cotton. Reverse of white cotton. Six red and six white strips. Quilting follows the strips in alternate fan and running feather.
c. 1870
Haydon Bridge, Northumberland
274 x 244 (108 x 96)
Donated by Mr D F Wadge
Acc.no.1972-658.126

105. Zigzag strippy
Turkey red, white and gold printed cotton. Reverse of white cotton. Nine strips of cream, five coloured zigzag strips applied along length of strips in zigzag and worm.
c. 1900
Haydon Bridge, Northumberland
269 x 180 (106 x 71}
Donated by Mr D F Wadge
Acc.no.1972-658.130

106. Mauve strippy
Printed coloured cotton and white cotton. Reverse of white cotton. Brown, mauve and yellow strips. Quilting follows the strips in twist, rose chain, running diamond and trail.
c. 1870
Haydon Bridge, Northumberland
226 x 185 (89 x 73)
Donated by Mr D F Wadge
Acc.no.1972-658.131

107. Pink and white strippy
Very pale pink and white cotton. Reverse of white cotton. Twelve strips. Quilting follows the strips in twist, running diamond, hammock and leaf.
c. 1900
Haydon Bridge, Northumberland
241 x 211 (95 x 83)
Donated by Mr D F Wadge
Acc.no.1972-658.132

108. Patchwork strippy
Multi-coloured cottons and green, pink and yellow cotton strips. Small pieced squares and diamonds in mauve, pale blue and pink. Other side of twelve strips. Quilting follows the strips in zigzag and twist.
c. 1916
Annfield Plain, Co. Durham
221 x 213 (87 x 84)
Donated by Mr J Peaden
Acc.no.1976-96.36

109. Wallsend strippy
Gold and blue printed cotton strips.
Reverse similar. Quilted outer border of
twist, otherwise quilting follows the strips
in worm, straight feather and bellows.
Made by Elizabeth Womphrey.
c. 1870
Wallsend, Newcastle upon Tyne
257 x 224 (101 x 88)
Donated by Mrs Mathewson
Acc.no.1977-161.2

110. Yellow and gold strippy
Yellow and gold cotton sateen. Reverse of
pink and peach cotton sateen. Five yellow
and four gold strips. The quilting follows
the strips in running diamond, plait,
rectangle, fan and swag.
c. 1900
Not known
241 x 213 (95 x 84)
Anonymous donation
Acc.no.1977-1256

111. Turkey red and white strippy
Turkey red and white cotton. Reverse of
white cotton. Five red and four white
strips. Quilted outer border of lines
enclosing chain, otherwise quilting follows
the strips in double hammock and running
diamond.
c. 1880
Not known
236 x 218 (93 x 86)
Anonymous donation
Acc.no.1977-1263

112. Mustard and cream strippy
Mustard and cream cotton sateen. Reverse
of dark pink cotton sateen. Five mustard
and four cream strips. Quilting follows the
strips and running diamond, fan, rose,
feather and diamond infill. Made by
Isabella Calvert.
c. 1899
Thornley, Co. Durham
229 x 196 (90 x 77)
Donated by Mrs B J Clark
Acc.no.1978-709.1

113. Turkey red and white strippy
Turkey red and white cotton. Reverse of
pink and white cotton. Five red and four
white strips in trail, twist, fan, feather and
running diamond with rose.
c.1899
Thornley, Co. Durham
234 x 206 (92 x 81)
Donated by Mrs B J Clark
Acc.no.1978-709.2

114. Blue and white strippy
Plain blue and white cotton with reverse of
blue floral cotton. Four blue and five white
strips. Quilting follows the strips in plait
and rings enclosing rose alternately.
c. 1910
Not known
234 x 208 (92 x 82)
Acquired
Acc.no.1978-1123.1

115. Mauve and cream strippy
Printed mauve and cream printed cotton.
Reverse of white cotton. Quilting follows
the strips in bellows and running diamond.
Made by Mrs Annie Roddam with the help
of three sisters.
c. 1906
Steel, Northumberland
241 x 218 (95 x 86)
Donated by Mrs Roddam
Acc.no.1980-505.1

116. Patchwork/strippy
Printed cottons in pink, blue, white, grey
and gold. Reverse of white cotton. Six
plain strips and five strips composed of
pieced squares on pink background.
Quilting follows the strips in twist and
running diamond.
1877
Consett, Co. Durham
231 x 208 (91 x 82)
Donated by Mr & Mrs A I Parker
Acc.no.1980-693

117. Peach/pink strippy
Peach pink sateen with reverse of pink
floral cotton. Quilting follows the strips in
twist, fan, bellows, running feather and
leaf.
c. 1912
Not known
221 x 196 (87 x 77)
Anonymous donation
Acc.no.1983-266.11

118. Pink and white strippy
Plain pink and printed cotton. Reverse of
white cotton. Five pink strips and four
white printed strips. Quilting follows strips
in zigzag and twist.
c. 1890
Not known
231 x 191 (91 x 75)
Anonymous donation
Acc.no.1984-73

119. Pink and green strippy
Pink and green cotton with printed paisley
cotton reverse and pink saw tooth edging
to reverse. The quilting follows the strips in
plait and twist alternatively.
c. 1900
Wolsingham
227 x 196 (89 x 77)
Acquired
Acc.no.1988-269

120. Shirtings strippy
Flannel shirtings in pastel colours in
varying widths of strip. Quilted in twist.
1900-10
Elsdon & Morpeth
232 x 170 (91 x 67)
Donated by Miss Wilde
Acc.no.1989-185

121. Pieced strippy
Blue & brown wool and twill fabrics in
strips. Two strips are pieced in squares and
triangles of alternating blue and grey
fabric. Three strips in alternating brown
and beige and cream stripes. The quilting
follows the pieced work in leaf & trail.
c. 1890-1900
Brampton, Cleveland
245 x 187 (96 x 74)
Acquired
Acc.no.1991-255

122. Cream and pink strippy
Cream and pink cotton with reverse of
cream & yellow cotton. Quilting follows
the strips in running feather and rose.
Made by Miss Elizabeth Beck of a lead-
mining family.
c. 1890-1900
Blanchland, Northumberland
236 x 201 (93 x 79)
Donated by Mrs Urwin
Acc.no.1993-4.1

123. Blue and white strippy
Blue & white cotton with reverse of printed
floral cotton. There are signs of pencil
marking on the strippy side. Quilting
follows the strips in trail. Made by Miss
Elizabeth Beck.
c. 1890-1900
Blanchland, Northumberland
231 x 201 (91 x 79)
Acquired
Acc.no.1993-4.3

124. Turkey red and white strippy
Turkey red and white cotton reversible
strippy quilt. Four red and five white strips,
reversing to five read and four white strips.
Quilted in zigzag, trail and worm.
c. 1890
Otterburn, Northumberland
259 x 245 (102 x 96)
Anonymous donation
Acc.no.1994-82

125. Blue and floral strippy
Pale blue cotton and printed floral cotton
with reverse of printed floral cotton. Five
blue strips alternating with four floral
strips. Quilted in strips of diamond and
feather. Made by Mrs Matilda Clish.
c. 1900-20
Annfield Plain, Co. Durham
191 x 157 (75 x 62)
Donated by Miss L. Clish
Acc.no.1994-121.4

126. Pastels strippy
Pastel cottons in blue, pink, yellow and white, pieced in very narrow 2" strips with reverse of pink printed cotton with blue printed borders. Quilted overall in scallop. Made by Mrs Matilda Clish.
c. 1900-20
Annfield Plain, Co. Durham
217 x 185 (85 x 73)
Donated by Miss L. Clish
Acc.no.1994-121.5

127. Blue and peach strippy
Pale blue and peach printed cotton strips, cream cotton reverse. Quilting follows the strips in running diamond, roses and fan. Made by Mrs Matilda Clish.
c. 1900-20
Annfield Plain, Co. Durham
226 x 196 (89 x 77)
Donated by Miss L Clish
Acc.no.1994-121.6

128. Shirtings strippy
Pink and white and blue & white checked cotton with reverse of white cotton. Four broad strips with four narrow strips in zigzag piecing. Outer printed cotton border. Quilted in strips of wave, worm, fan & hammock. Made by Elizabeth Teasdale of Riggside, St Johns Chapel (Gt grandmother of donor).
c. 1890
St. Johns Chapel, Weardale
236 x 226 (93 x 89)
Donated by Mrs A Glass
Acc.no.2000-90.1

129. Shirtings strippy
Pink and white and mauve & white checked cotton with reverse of white cotton. Outer printed cotton border. Alternating broad & narrow strips in pink & mauve in zigzag. Quilted in worm and twist. Made by Elizabeth Teasdale of Riggside, St Johns Chapel (Gt grandmother of donor).
c. 1890
St Johns Chapel, Weardale
236 x 234 (93 x 92)
Donated by Mrs A Glass
Acc.no.2000-90.2

130. Floral strippy
Printed floral cottons with reverse of cream cotton. Six dark floral strips contrast with six light floral strips. Quilting follows the strips and overlaps them.
c. 1910-20
County Durham
217 x 201 (85 x 79)
Anonymous donation
Acc.no.2004-136

131. Cummersdale strippy
Printed furnishing fabrics on both sides, roller printed by Stead McAlpin of Cummersdale, Carlisle. One broad central strip and two side contrasting strips, quilted overall in wineglass pattern. One design of iris with ribbon was dated 1895. Quilt made by Mrs Grace Irving of Silloth, Cumberland.
c. 1896-1906
Silloth, Cumberland
223 x 214 (88 x 84)
Acquired
Acc.no.2004-212

132. Peach and Cream Strippy
5 Peach and 4 cream cotton sateen strips and reverse of peach cotton sateen. The strips show the blue pencil marked design in feather, rose and horseshoe pattern, along the strips. The quilt was probably made by Miss Sarah Hunter Walker, (14/11/03 –11/7/74) of Annfield Plain, Co. Durham, the daughter of a miner.
c. 1930
Annfield Plain, Co. Durham
Donated by Mr John Walker
Acc.no.2006-146.1

PATCHWORK AND APPLIQUÉ QUILTS

133. Swaledale quilt
Printed and woven cotton shirtings. Reverse of pink and blue strips. Patchwork strips arranged around a central pink square. Quilted in strips in twist.
c. 1900
Grinton, N. Yorks
208 x 200 (82 x 79)
Donated by Mr F E Horn
Acc.no.1961-59a

134. Swaledale quilt
Printed cottons in pink, pale blue and cream. Reverse of cream cotton. Central pink windmill patchwork with outer border of pink saw tooth. Quilted in strips of twist.
c. 1890
Grinton, N. Yorks
229 x 186 (90 x 73)
Donated by Mr F E Horn
Acc.no.1961-59d

135. Bowes quilt
Printed cottons in white, blue, navy, pink and yellow. Reverse in strips of pink, blue and white. Series of assorted sized rectangles pieced around central square. Quilted in strips of trail, worm and bellows.
c. 1910
Spital, Bowes, N. Yorks
203 x 200 (80 x 79)
Donated by T J Alderson
Acc.no.1962-247

136. Bowes quilt
Colourful printed cottons in royal blue, Turkey red and pale striped fabrics. Reverse of striped cotton. Central yellow checked square around which are arranged an assortment of rectangles. Quilted in strips of twist.
c. 1910
Spital, Bowes, N. Yorks
210 x 188 (83 x 74)
Donated by T J Alderson
Acc.no.1962-247

137. Hexagon quilt
Pale printed cottons in mauve, blue, pink and white. Reverse of red and white chequered cotton. Quilted overall in diamond pattern.
c. 1870
Darlington, Co. Durham
240 x 214 (94 x 84)
Donated by Miss Chapman
Acc.no.1962-256

138. Sanderson baskets quilt
Plain pink and white cotton. Reverse of
white cotton. Pieced rows of patchwork
blocks containing baskets pieced from
triangular patches with applied handles.
Quilting follows the blocks in Weardale
chain border, baskets and flowers. Quilt
drawn by Elizabeth Sanderson.
1912
Allenheads, Northumberland
239 x 211 (94 x 83}
Donated by Mrs D Adamson
Acc.no.1963-56

139. Ovington quilt
Multi-coloured flannels and suitings.
Reverse of striped twill. Dazzling
patchwork design of square blocks pieced
together and outlined with black. Maroon
twill border. Quilted overall in wineglass.
Border of twist Made by Mrs Sybil Heslop.
c. 1900
Ovington, Northumberland
226 x 214 (89 x 84)
Donated by Mr R Graham
Acc.no.1963-136

140. Ovington quilt
Multi-coloured flannels and suitings.
Reverse of similar material in pieced
squares. Startling design of pieced
octagons in light and dark colours with
bottle green border. Quilted overall in
wineglass border of twist. Made by Mrs
Sybil Heslop.
c. 1900
Ovington, Northumberland
226 x 214 (89 x 84)
Donated by Mr R Graham
Acc.no.1963-137

141. Askrigg quilt
Multi-coloured printed cottons. Reverse of
white cotton. Central pieced windmill
design framed with squares and rectangles.
Quilted in overall diamond pattern.
c. 1880
Thornton Rust, N. Yorks
222 x 216 (87 x 85)
Acquired from farm sale
Acc.no.1963-448

142. North Shields quilt
Printed cottons in blue, pink, beige, gold
and white. Reverse of white cotton. Quilt
consists of small pieced octagons. Quilted
in strips of twist, bellows, worm and
running diamond.
c. 1870
North Shields, Northumberland
242 x 224 (95 x 88)
Donated by Mrs M Forster
Acc.no.1966-217

143. Framed quilt
Brightly coloured printed cottons. Reverse
of white cotton, central printed square
surrounded by strips and squares. Quilted
in centre with roses surrounded by zigzag
twist and diamond infill.
c. 1900
Durham
259 x 231 (102 x 91)
Donated by Mrs Foss
Acc.no.1967-894

144. Barnard Castle quilt
Pale printed cottons. Reverse of white
cotton. Diagonally set pieced squares of
striped cotton and pieced squares of small
patchwork in pink, white and beige.
Quilted in diamonds and leaves.
c. 1880
Barnard Castle, Co. Durham
261 x 254 (103 x 100)
Donated by Miss F M Storey
Acc.no.1967-920.1

145. Gretna Green quilt
Multi-coloured printed cottons. Reverse of
white cotton. Patchwork of many very tiny
hexagons in blocks of 7 on white
background. Border of triangles and strips.
Yellow frill. Only the border is quilted in
zigzag. Made by Margaret Isabella
Mitchell.
c. 1856
Gretna Green, Dumfriesshire
254 x 231 (100 x 91)
Donated by Miss E Mitchell
Acc.no.1967-939

146. Chintz wedding quilt
Multi-coloured chintzes in pieced squares.
Reverse of white cotton. Very fine quilting
in squares around a central true lover's
knot. The quilting follows the patchwork.
Probably made as a wedding quilt.
c. 1840s-1910
Walbottle, Northumberland
268 x 260 (106 x 102)
Donated by Miss A J Winspear
Acc.no.1968-94

147. Irish Chain quilt
Turkey red, green and white cotton.
Reverse of white cotton. Irish four patch
chain of red and green squares on white
background. Quilted overall in diamond.
Border on two sides of running feather.
c. 1890
North Shields, Northumberland
214 x 198 (84 x 78)
Donated by Miss H I Nichol
Acc.no.1968-166.1

148. Wensleydale quilt
Coloured printed cottons in beige, pink
and red paisley. Reverse of white cotton.
Central red paisley square around which
are set rectangular strips-medallion style.
Quilted overall in wineglass.
c. 1880
Carperby, N. Yorks
249 x 214 (98 x 84)
Donated by Miss A Scott
Acc.no.1969-276.1

149. Feathered star quilt
Printed floral material in reds, beige and
blue, on white background. Reverse of
white cotton. Nine, eight pointed, pieced
feathered stars, saw tooth border and
pieced zigzag edging. Quilting does not
follow patchwork.
c. 1890
Not known
204 x 204 (80 x 80)
Anonymous donation
Acc.no.1971-16.2

150. Patchwork quilt
Multi-coloured printed cottons. Reverse of
cream cotton. Assorted pieced squares and
rectangles in pinks, beige and striped
material with a printed strip down each
long edge. Quilting in strips of diamond
and twist.
c. 1870s
Not known
229 x 178 (94 x 70)
Anonymous donation
Acc.no.1971-16.8

151. Framed quilt
Multi-coloured printed cottons in pale
colours. Reverse of printed cotton. Centre
square of red and white checks around
which are arranged strips of pieced
material. Squares set at corners. Quilting
follows the patchwork in trail, diamond
and plait.
c. 1870
Not known
216 x 216 (85 x 85)
Anonymous donation
Acc.no.1971-16.11

152. Pink star quilt
Faded pink and white cotton. Reverse of
white cotton. Central eight pointed pieced
star in pink on white background with
three pink and two white borders to outer
edge. Quilting follows patchwork in twist,
wave and rose, leaf and running feather.
Quilt made by ladies of a church
sewing/quilting club.
c. 1914
Springwell, Newcastle
221 x 196 (87 x 77)
Donated by Mrs L Shore
Acc.no.1971-265

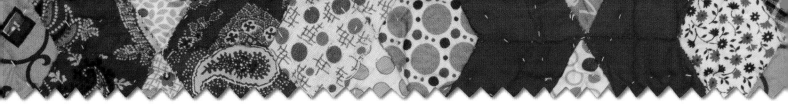

153. Hexagon quilt
Multi-coloured printed cotton. Reverse of white cotton. Many tiny pieced hexagons on white background. Reds, mauves, gold, beige etc. 'Number of patches 7527, Date 1878' – marked on reverse. Outer border only quilted, in twist.
1878
Riding Mill, Northumberland
267 x 234 (105 x 92)
Donated by Mrs Logan
Acc.no.1971-371

154. Framed quilt
Multi-coloured printed cottons in browns, beige, blue and mauve. Reverse of white cotton. Central eight-pointed star around which are arranged pieced strips. Quilting consists of border of twist and infill of wineglass. Made by Mrs Sarah Atkinson.
Pre 1890
Kirby Thore, Westmorland
239 x 211 (94 x 83)
Donated by Miss C Brown
Acc.no.1972-210.42.2

155. Sanderson pink star quilt
Pink and white cotton. Reverse of white cotton. Large eight pointed pink star with three pink and two white borders. Quilt marking can be seen. Quilted in twist, rose and leaf and diamond infill. Quilt almost certainly marked by Elizabeth Sanderson or an apprentice.
c. 1900
Allenheads, Northumberland
226 x 226 (89 x 89)
Donated by Mr D F Wadge
Acc.no.1972-658.117

156. Chintz basket quilt
Chintzes with reverse of white cotton. Medallion style. Central printed panel of basket of flowers in wreath, possibly late 18th century, surrounded by alternate pieced windmills, and borders of chintz. Very likely made by Joe the Quilter of Warden.
c. 1820s
Haydon Bridge, Northumberland
246 x 236 (97 x 93)
Donated by Mr D F Wadge
Acc.no.1972-658.120

157. Octagon quilt
Multi-coloured printed cottons with reverse of white cotton. Many small pieced octagons in purples, mauve, red, pink and brown, pieced with small squares between. Wide strip border all round of plain printed material. Quilted in strips of bellows, trail and ring chain.
c. 1880/5
Haydon Bridge, Northumberland
5251 x 216 (99 x 85)
Donated by Mr D F Wadge
Acc.no.1972-658.127

158. Patchwork squares quilt
Multi-coloured printed material with reverse of white calico. Quilt made up of squares pieced together with outer border of striped material. Simply quilted in straight diagonals radiating from centre to each corner.
c. 1900
Haydon Bridge, Northumberland
196 x 163 (77 x 64)
Donated by Mr D F Wadge
Acc.no.1972-658.128

159. Flannel basket quilt
Brilliantly coloured flannels and suitings. Reverse of plain woollen material. Central royal blue square on which is appliquéd basket. Bright squares and strips in Turkey red, grey and purple and bottle green. Very simply quilted following patchwork. Made by Mrs Ann Shanks.
c. 1910
Benwell, Newcastle upon Tyne
211 x 150 (83 x 59)
Donated by Mrs M Irvine
Acc.no.1973-517

160. Framed quilt
Coloured plain and printed cottons. Reverse of white cotton. Tiny pieced squares worked from centre nine patch square, in borders of colour, quilted in hammock and leaf with fern infill.
c. 1870
Newcastle upon Tyne
254 x 246 (100 x 97)
Donated by Mrs Potts
Acc.no.1973-518

161. Framed quilt
Printed cottons in mauve, beige and pink, reverse of cream cotton. Large central square composed of pieced hexagons in blocks of seven on mauve background. Outer strip borders. Quilted in zigzag, twist and bellows.
c. 1900
Stanley, Co. Durham
257 x 244 (101 x 96)
Donated by Mrs W Rollins
Acc.no.1974-76

162. Whitfield quilt
Multi-coloured printed cottons. Reverse of white cotton, pieced octagons with white square centre. Kansas dugout pattern, outer strip border. Quilted in running feather and flowers. Made by Elizabeth Jane Newbegin.
c. 1865
Whitfield, Northumberland
262 x 249 (103 x 98)
Donated by Miss Eva Reay
Acc.no.1975-265

163. Princess Feather appliqué quilt
Turkey red and white cotton. Reverse of white cotton. Large machine stitched appliquéd central flower in red with outer leaves and stars. Outer red border. Quilted in strips of plait, worm, running feather, flower and fan. Made by Mrs Goldsborough for wedding of Isabella Levitt.
c. 1895
Pelton, Co. Durham
241 x 211 (95 x 83)
Donated by Mrs Bell
Acc.no.1976-821.4

164. Patchwork star quilt
Brilliantly coloured printed cottons, some dating c. 1840s, 1860s and 1870s. Reverse of small scale madder print c.1920s/30s. Pieced diamonds form all over star pattern. Use of Turkey red to outline stars. Quilting in strips of worm and trail. Made by Isabella Womphrey.
c. 1930s
Willington Quay, Newcastle
229 x 203 (90 x 80)
Donated by Mrs Mathewson
Acc.no.1977-161.1

165. Chequerboard quilt
Turkey red and light printed materials. Reverse of white cotton. Overall alternate red and light coloured squares giving chequerboard effect. Two lattice strips across quilt. Quilting in zigzag.
c. 1860
Carlisle, Cumberland
206 x 198 (82 x 78)
Donated by the Misses Buxton
Acc.no.1977-933.1

166. Framed quilt
Printed cottons in gold, beige and muted colours. Reverse of white cotton. Central square composed of four triangles surrounded by borders of strips and triangles to outer edge. Simple quilting in zigzag.
c. 1850
Carlisle, Cumberland
218 x 196 (86 x 77)
Donated by the Misses Buxton
Acc.no.1977-993.2

167. Framed quilt
Pale plain and printed cottons. Reverse of cotton strips. Central design of eight triangles forming a square in pink and blue, surrounded by patchwork strips. Quilting in twist, not very effective.
c. 1890
Not known
244 x 224 (96 x 88)
Anonymous donation
Acc.no.1977-1240

168. Hexagon quilt
Coloured printed cottons with reverse of pale blue cotton. Tiny hexagons in groups of seven. Random arrangement of colours. White border. Quilting in leaf and diamond.
c. 1870
Not known
221 x 170 (87 x 67)
Anonymous donation
Acc.no.1977-1243

169. Framed quilt
Colourful printed cotton with reverse of white cotton. Centre square of twenty five pieced stars surrounded by pieced strips of squares, rectangles and T shapes in browns, mauve, red and white, outer border of plain striped material. Quilting in wineglass.
c. 1815-1860
Not known
244 x 234 (96 x 92)
Acc.no.1977-1244

170. Patchwork quilt
Cotton sateen in bright pink, yellow, navy and white. Reverse of cotton strips. Centre composed of pieced squares surrounded by irregular strips placed at random. Quilting in strips of trail and worm.
c. 1930
Not known
191 x 150 (75 x 59)
Acc.no.1977-1245

171. Framed quilt
Printed cottons in beige, browns, cream, gold and pink. Some fabrics date c.1820s and 1840s. Reverse of cream cotton. Central square enclosing nine pieced squares, surrounded by strips and pieced borders. One outer border of wild goose chase. Quilted overall in wineglass.
c. 1865
Not known
236 x 229 (93 x 90)
Anonymous donation
Acc.no.1977-1262

172. Patchwork/Applique quilt
Plain white, pink and green cotton. Pink floral printed reverse. Nine appliqué flowers with many other small applied pink and white dots overall. Border of white wild goose chase on green border. Outer border of pink rectangles. Quilted overall. Very faded and badly worn.
c. 1870
Lumley, Co. Durham
229 x 224 (90 x 88)
Donated by Mr N Wilson
Acc.no.1978-1029.1

173. Hexagon quilt
Turkey red and colourful printed cottons. Reverse of cream cotton. Turkey red hexagons and printed hexagons in blue, mauve and grey on cream background. Outer border of red hexagons. Quilted in bell, twist, bellows and wineglass. Made by Mrs Margaret Wallace for her wedding.
c. 1870
Beltingham, Northumberland
257 x 229 (101 x 90)
Donated by Mrs Suthrien
Acc.no.1979-795

174. Turkey red star quilt
Turkey red and white pieced top. Reverse of white cotton. Eight pointed star enclosing another star. Alternate red and white borders. A favourite design of Elizabeth Sanderson whose work this almost certainly is. Quilted in Weardale chain, running feather and twist.
c. 1890
Allenheads, Northumberland
229 x 226 (90 x 89)
Acquired
Acc.no.1980-884.1

175. Irish Chain quilt
Turkey red, pink and beige printed cotton, on cream cotton sateen. Reverse of cream sateen. One patch Irish chain in faded reds and pinks. Quilting in strips of twist, running diamond and trail.
c. 1880
Houghton-le-Side, Co. Durham
246 x 216 (97 x 85)
Donated by Mrs M Cockburn
Acc.no.1981-3

176. Pink and white baskets quilt
Pink and white cotton, reverse of white cotton. Overall pattern of baskets pieced from small pink triangles with appliquéd handles. White background, quilted overall in diamond.
c. 1870
Not known
183 x 168 (72 x 66)
Acquired
Acc.no.1981-143

177. Four-leafed clover quilt
Pink and green cotton sateen. Reverse of floral cotton sateen. Central four leafed clover in green on pink background. Three green and two pink borders. Finely quilted in twist, running feather and plait. Very similar in style to Allenheads quilts. Made by Mrs Lumsden for granddaughter's wedding.
1916
Craghead, Co. Durham
203 x 191 (80 x 75)
Donated by Mr Bethwaite
Acc.no.1981-303

178. Block quilt
Green, cream and yellow cotton sateens. Reverse of cream cotton sateen. Pieced block quilt made up of squares with pieced diagonal leaves giving impression of circles. Quilting follows patchwork. Made by Mrs Matilda Clish.
1907-14
Annfield Plain, Co. Durham
224 x 183 (88 x 72)
Donated by Miss Clish
Acc.no.1981-365.1

179. Block quilt
Yellow and cream cotton sateen. Pieced block design similar to Cat.no.143 except with plain border quilted in running feather with cream block in each corner. Made by Mrs Matilda Clish.
1907-14
Annfield Plain, Co. Durham
216 x 175 (85 x 69)
Donated by Miss Clish
Acc.no.1981-365.2

180. Turkey Tracks quilt
Red, green and white cotton. Reverse of white cotton. Nine pieced blocks with stylised leaves applied to each joined by Turkey red strips and green squares. Outer zigzag border. Quilted overall in zigzag. Made by Mrs Morphet.
c. 1912
Kirkby Stephen, Westmorland
236 x 213 (93 x 84)
Acquired
Acc.no.1982-118

181. Framed quilt
Plain pink, white and pale printed cottons. Reverse of white cotton. Central square of triangles placed in squares with Turkey red edging. Outer borders of squares and triangles many of which outlined with red. Outer plain printed border, overall quilting in diamonds and leaves. Made by Mrs Elizabeth Robinson.
c. 1907
Newcastle upon Tyne
229 x 224 (90 x 88)
Donated by Mrs Robinson
Acc.no.1982-227

182. Flower appliqué quilt
Red, orange, green and white cotton. Reverse of white cotton, four large appliqué flowers in red and orange with green leaves. Red and orange saw tooth borders. Outer plain green border. Quilting in trail, diamond twist and following patchwork. Made by Mrs Phoebe Watson.
c. 1860-70
Ireshopeburn, Co. Durham
206 x 186 (81 x 73)
Acquired
Acc.no.1982-243

183. Star of Bethlehem quilt
Red, orange and green and white cotton.
Reverse of white cotton. Eight-pointed star
made up on tiny diamonds in orange, red
and green on white background. Small star
at each point of large star. Stars are
appliquéd by machine. Quilting in small
flowers and large feathers. Diamond infill.
c. 1870
Weardale, Co. Durham
257 x 254 (101 x 100)
Acquired
Acc.no.1982-244

184. Red and white baskets quilt
Turkey red and white cotton. Reverse of
white cotton. Overall pattern of baskets
pieced from small red triangles, handles
applied. Quilted in wineglass.
c. 1880
Keswick, Cumberland
224 x 191 (88 x 75)
Acquired
Acc.no.1982-295

185. Turkey red border quilt
Turkey red and white cotton. Reverse of
white cotton. Central double E shape
surrounded by four red and four white
borders. Quilted overall in zigzag.
c. 1870
Kirkby Stephen, Westmorland
206 x 170 (81 x 67)
Acquired
Acc.no.1982-296

186. Cot quilt
Grey and white striped and white cotton.
Reverse of white cotton. Chequerboard
effect of alternate grey and white squares.
Quilted in worm and running diamond.
c. 1890
Blackhill, Co. Durham
84 x 69 (33 x 27)
Donated by Mrs Stoddard
Acc.no.1983-226

187. Turkey red Irish chain quilt
Turkey red and white cotton. Reverse of
white cotton. Irish chain consisting of large
red squares linked with two smaller
squares. Outer red and white border. Fine
quilting follows the patchwork.
c. 1870
Northumberland
241 x 221 (95 x 87)
Acquired
Acc.no.1983-234

188. Flowerpot appliqué quilt
Printed red, plain green and white cotton.
Reverse of white cotton. Central flowerpot
with flowers appliquéd within green
framed square. Stars and buds appliquéd in
white and green on red background.
Alternate outer borders of white and red.
Flowerpot in each corner. Made by Mrs
Isabella Cruddas.
c. 1870-80
Rookhope, Co. Durham
234 x 234 (92 x 92)
Acquired
Acc.no.1984-70

189. Blue star quilt
Blue and white pieced cotton sateen top.
White cotton reverse. Probably stamped
by Elizabeth Sanderson. Quilted in
Weardale chain, running feather and twist.
c. 1890
Allenheads, Northumberland
234 x 224 (92 x 88)
Donated by Mr & Mrs Allison
Acc.no.1985-148

190. Patchwork quilt
Pieced centre of multi-coloured printed
cotton hexagons on printed floral ground.
Quilted overall in wave design. Machined
edges.
c. 1907
Seaton Burn, Northumberland
243 x 193 (96 x 76)
Donated by Mrs Crozier
Acc.no.1985-221

191. Patchwork quilt
Pieced quilt in white cotton and small
design printed cotton. Central diagonally
set square. Finally quilted – worn sides
folded in.
c. 1860
Woodburn, Northumberland
249 x 189 (98 x 74)
Donated by Mrs Hunt
Acc.no.1985-317

192. Patchwork/appliqué quilt
Blue and white cotton pieced top. Rows
of blue baskets and double blue strip
borders on white ground. Quilted overall
with roses in squares. Twist and feather
borders.
c. 1920
Mickley, Co. Durham
240 x 203 (94 x 80)
Donated by Mr Bates
Acc.no.1985-336.1

193. Patchwork quilt
Pieced quilt of pink, blue and cream
squares set side-by-side and set diagonally.
Quilting follows the patchwork squares
and lozenges.
c. 1924
Mickleton, Co. Durham
243 x 213 (96 x 84)
Donated by Mrs A J Cowling
Acc.no.1985-356.1

194. Cot quilt
Pieced squares and triangles in printed
cottons, in pinks, mauves and beiges.
Quilted overall in twist.
c. 1895
Mickleton, Co. Durham
98 x 79 (39 x 31)
Donated by Mrs A J Cowling
Acc.no.1985-356.4

195. Bible Quilt
Quilt of Turkey red cotton and light printed
floral material with reverse of white cotton.
Printed texts on cotton, same with
illustrations, have been machine appliquéd
onto a Turkey red background. The whole
quilt is crudely hand quilted.
c. 1880-90
Barningham, Richmond, N. Yorks
213 x 203 (84 x 80)
Acquired
Acc.no.1986-42

196. Green pieced star quilt
Quilt of green and white cotton. The quilt
is made up of 16 pieced green stars set on
a white background with zigzag border.
The quilting is very fine and follows the
patchwork. Quilt came from the home of
Mrs Reed whose people were grocers in
Pity Me, Durham.
c. 1880
Pity Me, Durham
241 x 229 (95 x 90)
Donated by Mrs Ella Stothard
Acc.no.1986-259

197. Drunkard's Path quilt
Turkey red and white cotton with reverse
of white cotton. The pieced design has
gone a little awry but is effective. Quilting
in strips of diamond, flower and wineglass.
c. 1880
Burnopfield, Co. Durham
253 x 193 (100 x 76)
Donated by Mrs Dent
Acc.no.1986-293

198. Turkey red and white patchwork quilt

Patchwork quilt of Turkey red and white triangles with reverse of white cotton. Quilted in strips of twist. Made in Heckmondwike near Leeds, by Mrs Mary Pearson.
c. 1900
Heckmondwike
237 x 225 (93 x 89)
Donated by Mrs Mabel Duxbury
Acc.no.1987-104

199. Framed printed centre quilt

Multicoloured printed cotton squares are set around a printed floral centrepiece. The quilt includes some early fabrics dating between 1810 up to the late 1820s. The quilting follows the pieced work.
c. 1829/30
Teesdale, Co. Durham
293 x 254 (115 x 100)
Acquired
Acc.no.1989-395

200. Turkey red and white quilt

Eight narrow Turkey red cotton strips are set on a white cotton background with an outer border of Turkey red. Reverse of floral printed cotton. The quilting follows the strips in zigzag, trail, and rose. The quilt was made by Miss Catherine Rea and her sisters of Poplar Street, S. Moor, Stanley – a mining family.
c. 1910
Stanley, Co. Durham
228 x 185 (90 x 73)
Donated by Mr & Mrs A Gibbons
Acc.no.1990-265

201. Early Hearts Quilt

Pieced and appliqué framed quilt in printed cottons. Centre square of applied stylised flowers set as diamond in central square border of white hearts on a red background. Appliqué flowers in corners. Outer border of appliqué leaves and flowers – very ornate design. Reverse of white cotton. Some interesting and early printed cottons dating between 1825 and late 1830s.
c. 1830s
Weardale, o. Durham
270 x 250 (106 x 98)
Acquired
Acc.no.1990-282

202. Princess Charlotte framed quilt

Pieced framed quilt in printed cottons. Centre panel with words 'Princess Charlotte of Wales married Leopold Prince of Saxecobourg May 2 1816'. Centre surrounded by arrangement of printed cotton squares pieced alternatively with pink fabric and printed floral fabric. Outer border on two sides of pink/blue trail with feather. Reverse of white cotton. Quilted overall. The quilt was made by Mrs Anne Greenwell, mother of George Greenwell, founder of Greenwell & Sons, Grocers at Silver Street, Durham. Quilt made for her son Anthony Greenwell who was baptised 23rd June 1815 at St. Andrews, Auckland.
c. 1830
Bishop Auckland, Co. Durham
230 x 230 (91 x 91)
Donated by Mrs P B West
Acc.no.1991-148

203. Grandmother's flower garden

Bright multi-coloured printed cotton hexagons pieced around a central hexagon. Careful arrangement with Turkey red predominating. Outer printed two colour border. Reverse in strips of cotton. Made for Miss Mary Selby for her 21st birthday in 1881.
1881
Hartlepool
183 x 183 (72 x 72)
Donated by Miss Vera Oldham
Acc.no.1991-230

204. Turkey red & white star quilt

Red and white cotton with reverse in white cotton. Central red eight-pointed star within white eight-pointed star set on red background with alternating red and white borders. Quilting follows the pieced work in running diamond, roses and leaves. Quilt made by Margaret Earsdon for her wedding.
c. 1915-20
Shankhouse, Cramlington, Northumberland
224 x 207 (88 x 81)
Anonymous donor
Acc.no.1992-106

205. Irish chain patchwork quilt

Pink, yellow and cream cotton with white cotton reverse. Outer plain borders of pink and yellow fabric with double Irish chain in yellow & pink set on the cream background. Quilted in bellows and rose pattern.
c. 1910
Gosforth, Newcastle upon Tyne
233 x 222 (92 x 87)
Donated by Mrs Grace Elliot
Acc.no.1993-170

206. Pink and blue pieced star quilt

Plain pink, blue and white cotton fabrics with reverse of white cotton. Pieced white stars are joined by strips of pink cotton to form a lattice pattern set on a blue background. The quilting follows the pieced design in roses, diamonds and leaves.
c. 1900-10
Weardale, Co. Durham
230 x 223 (90 x 84)
Acquired
Acc.no.1993-178

207. Mary Fairless's star quilt

Mauve and white cotton with reverse of white cotton. Typical Sanderson star pattern. The mauve fabric was called Zephyr and purchased from Allendale Co-op. The quilt was made by Mary Fairless, pupil of Mrs J Peart, the first that she completed at the age of 21 years. Quilted in twist and running feather.
1929
Allendale, Northumberland
235 x 230 (92 x 90)
Acquired
Acc.no.1993-212

208. Turkey red and white patchwork quilt

Turkey red and white cotton hexagons arranged in alternating borders around a central red hexagon. Outer white border with red squares in each corner. Reverse of white cotton. Quilted in twist on borders.
c. 1910-20
Teesdale, Co. Durham
207 x 196 (81 x 77)
Acquired
Acc.no.1993-253

209. Methodist signature quilt

Turkey red and white cotton with reverse of white cotton. Central red square with '1894 Zion Chapel Methodist New Connection Sheriff Hill' embroidered in cream chain stitch. The quilt is made up of alternating red and white triangles pieced together, each with an embroidered signature of a member of the chapel.
1894
Gateshead, Co. Durham
259 x 245 (102 x 96)
Donated by Mrs M Bell
Acc.no.1994-31

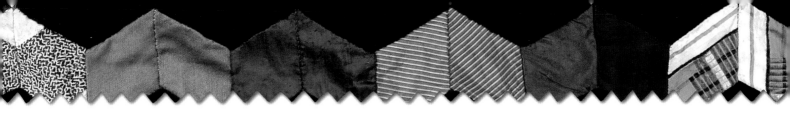

210. Patchwork quilt
Multi-coloured plain pastel & printed cottons with faded printed cotton reverse. Pieced pattern – Robbing Peter to pay Paul. Quilting follows the pieced work in leaf pattern. Made by Mrs Matilda Clish.
c. 1900-20
Annfield Plain, Co. Durham
219 x 175 (86 x 69)
Donated by Miss L. Clish
Acc.no.1994-121.2

211. Patchwork and appliqué starburst quilt
Turkey red, yellow and white cotton with reverse of white cotton. Central eight pointed yellow star surrounded by alternating circles of diamonds in red, white and yellow. Outer red, white and yellow borders. Quilting in diamond with outer rose and feather border. Quilt made by Jane Hole, from a mining family. She used to take part in Women's Bright Hour at West Pelton Methodist Chapel.
c. 1920-30
East Stanley, Co. Durham
256 x 255 (101 x 100)
Donated by Mrs Flynn
Acc.no.1994-202

212. Patchwork star quilt
Red, cream and cotton fabric with reverse of white. Nine stars in pieced diamonds in red and cream are set across the quilt on the white background. Outer borders in red, white and cream. Quilting follows the pieced work in feather wreath and diamond.
c. 1900
Gateshead
217 x 211 (85 x 83)
Acquired
Acc.no.1997-18

213. Hexhamshire framed quilt
Pink, blue, gold and printed cottons with reverse of white cotton and pink bound edges. Central pieced pink & blue flower set on white square within larger pink square. Zigzag pieced borders of blue on gold alternating with pink. Quilted with rose, running feather and diamond infill following the pieced design. Made by one of the Thompson family who came originally from Hexhamshire.
c. 1890
Westgate in Weardale
253 x 242 (100 x 95)
Donated by the Misses Thompson
Acc.no.1999-58.1

214. Turkey red and white star quilt
Pieced quilt of Turkey red and white cotton with reverse of white cotton. Overall pieced stars, consisting of white square set with eight triangle points on white background. Outer red diamond border, set at an angle. Quilted overall in diamond. Made by one of the Thompson family, originally from Hexhamshire.
c. 1890
Westgate in Weardale
248 x 243 (98 x 96)
Donated by the Misses Thompson
Acc.no.1999-58.2

215. Crazy patchwork quilt
Multi-coloured silks, satins and velours pieced together in crazy design with herringbone stitching. Reverse of yellow satin with yellow frill all round. Very gaudy and colourful. Individual pieces have been embroidered with fancy stitches, butterflies, cats, names and dated 1926, Grove House. Quilted overall in diamond. Made by Maria Armstrong.
1926
Blackhill, Consett, Co. Durham
218 x 197 (86 x 77)
Donated by Mr I Armstrong
Acc.no.2001-41.2

216. Tumbling boxes quilt
Multi-coloured cottons with printed cotton reverse. The quilt is composed of an overall tumbling box pattern. The quilting follows the pieced pattern. The quilt was made by Martha Best, who had been in service at Sadberge Hall.
c. 1910
Sadberge, Darlington, Co. Durham
236 x 217 (93 x 85)
Donated by Mrs Best
Acc.no.2002-159.1

217.Green star patchwork
Green and white cotton with white cotton reverse. Green pieced stars spaced evenly on a white background. Outer green border with white squares. Quilting follows the pieced work in circles enclosing roses. Made by a member of the Emerson or Lonsdale family.
c. 1870-1900
St Johns Chapel, Weardale
231 x 207 (91 x 81)
Donated by Mrs R Chamberlain & Mr H Lonsdale
Acc.no.2003-156

218. Turkey red and white basket quilt
Turkey red and white cotton with white cotton reverse. Block pieced overall design of red baskets pieced from triangles with applied handles on a white background. Quilting follows the pieced work in rose and diamond. Made by grandmother of donor.
c. 1900
Castleside, Co. Durham
234 x 222 (92 x 87)
Donated by Mr T A Pearson
Acc.no.2004-19.1

219. Irish chain quilt
Printed mauve cotton on white cotton background with reverse of white cotton. Pattern of single Irish chain in small & larger mauve squares. The quilting follows the pieced work in circles enclosing diamond infill. Made by grandmother of donor.
c. 1900
Castleside, Co. Durham
264 x 264 (104 x 104)
Donated by Mr T A Pearson
Acc.no.2004-19.2

220. Patchwork/Applique quilt
Printed cotton fabrics, pieced in large squares with detailed appliqué on alternate squares. Central square has embroidered 'J.A.Blenkinsop Born on the 2 of June in the year 1839 ad'.
Reverse of white cotton. Made probably c. 1850s.
Stockton on Tees
240 x 223 (94 x 88)
Donated by Mr.and Mrs.G.W.Barker
Acc. no. 2006-206

COVERLETS

221. Tumbling blocks coverlet
Multi-coloured silks. Reverse of purple woollen material. Small silk patches in block pattern, mauves, blue and black predominated. Not quilted.
c. 1900
Consett, Co. Durham
213 x 213 (84 x 84)
Donated by Miss K M Grainger
Acc.no.1966-3

222. Cot coverlet
Multicoloured woven brocades and furnishing fabrics, manufactured sample pieces stitched together in rectangles, on both sides, one possibly by Voysey.
c. 1900-5
Mickleton, Teesdale
110 x 69 (43 x 27)
Donated by Mrs T Dent
Acc.no.1967-176

223. Cot Coverlet
Red cotton paisley print and other pale printed cottons. Reverse of white cotton. Pieced hexagons in pale prints with red centres. Red paisley border. Not quilted.
c. 1900
Barnard Castle, Co. Durham
102 x 102 (40 x 40)
Donated by Miss F M Storey
Acc.no.1967-920.5

224. Crazy coverlet
Multi-coloured printed cottons, beige, white, brown and sepia. No reverse. Carefully pieced centre in small diamonds and outer stars. Outer area made up of large irregular "crazy" patches. Not quilted.
c. 1900
Yorkshire
234 x 219 (92 x 86)
Donated by Mr & Miss Cruttenden
Acc.no.1969-188

225. Honeycomb coverlet
Small hexagons joined by feather stitch making thirteen large hexagons in honeycomb pattern. Maroon border, and maroon, green and yellow on white background. Not quilted.
1966-70
Carlton, N. Yorks
377 x 198 (148 x 78)
Donated by Mrs E Gardner
Acc.no.1970-510

226. Diamond coverlet
Coloured printed cottons, red paisley, pink, green, blue on pale background. Reverse of printed cotton. Small hexagons pieced to form diamonds arranged symmetrically. Not quilted.
c. 1880
Not known
264 x 204 (104 x 80)
Anonymous donation
Acc.no.1971-16.1

227. Unfinished coverlet
Printed cottons in blue, pink, brown and white. No reverse. Small hexagons pieced to form larger hexagons all still with original papers, some dated 1841 and 1855. Made by an elderly countrywoman. Not quilted.
1860-70
Allenheads, Northumberland
218 x 193 (86 x 76)
Donated by Mr H E Ruddock
Acc.no.1971-129

228. Embroidered coverlet
Blue, scarlet and beige cottons with white lace edging. Reverse of beige sateen. Strips of material in latticework with applied flowers and leaves. Outer borders of alternate blue and scarlet. Not quilted.
c. 1870
Durham
259 x 254 (102 x 100)
Donated by Mrs Hopkins
Acc.no.1972-629

229. Honeycomb coverlet
Multi-coloured printed cottons, pale pink, grey, beige and gold. Reverse of white cotton. Small hexagons pieced to form larger hexagons in all over honeycomb effect. Not quilted.
c. 1870
Satley, Co. Durham
241 x 234 (95 x 92)
Donated by Mrs B Stephenson
Acc.no.1972-640

230. Tumbling blocks coverlet
Multi-coloured brilliant silks in black, yellow and other colours. No reverse material. Tumbling box pattern. Unfinished and not quilted.
c. 1900
Ravenglass, Cumberland
224 x 191 (88 x 75)
Donated by Dr M Timperley
Acc.no.1972-695

231. Embroidered coverlet
Multi-coloured silks on black background. Reverse of orange cotton. Central square with embroidered wreath. Other pieced squares individually embroidered. Outer border has verses of 'Jesu lover of my soul' embroidered. 'Done by Ann Johnson aged 78 1883'
1883
Hartlepool, Co. Durham
224 x 206 (88 x 81)
Donated by Mrs Phalp
Acc.no.1973-273

232. Patchwork/ appliqué coverlet
Printed cottons in beige, pink and mauve and plain white cotton. Reverse of white cotton. Large central square of white cotton onto which is appliquéd large flower, small stars and wreaths. The pieced squares surround this and there is an outer strip border.
c. 1860
Wallsend, Newcastle
244 x 229 (96 x 90)
Donated by Mrs Matthewson
Acc.no.1977-161.3

233. Patchwork coverlet
Multi-coloured printed cottons set in borders around central pieced star. Narrow borders of pieced triangles and squares. Coverlet not quilted. Probably originated in Lincolnshire.
c. 1890
Newcastle upon Tyne
254 x 188 (100 x 74)
Donated by Mrs Kington
Acc.no.1977-996

234. Framed coverlet
Multi-coloured printed cottons – brown, beige and golds. No reverse material. Central square surrounded by borders of triangles, strips and 'wild goose chase' pattern. Not quilted.
c. 1910
Not known
264 x 264 (104 x 104)
Anonymous donation
Acc.no.1977-1258

235. Patchwork coverlet
Multi-coloured silks, satins and velvets. No reverse material. Pieced hexagons. Unfinished coverlet.
c. 1870/80
Kirk Merrington, Co. Durham
175 x 147 (69 x 58)
Donated by Miss McMahon
Acc.no.1978-879.1

236. Crazy coverlet
Multi-coloured printed cottons. Reverse of beige cotton twill. Irregular sized piece of cotton in assorted shapes all over. No definite pattern. No quilting.
c. 1880
Whitley Bay, Northumberland
201 x 185 (79 x 73)
Donated by Mr Jackson
Acc.no.1978-884.2

237. Fuffly coverlet
White cotton on both sides. Small hexagonal patches, material gathered to create rosette effect. Made by children at mothers' quilting sessions.
c. 1870
Ebchester, Co. Durham
124 x 122 (49 x 48)
Donated by Mrs M. Burn
Acc.no.1983-35

238. Crazy coverlet

Multi-coloured silks, satins and velvets.
Central star enclosed square of crazy
pieces. One border of crazy pieces and
outer border of squares and triangle.
Made by Hannah Elizabeth Scott.
c. 1890
Waldridge Fell, Co. Durham
218 x 218 (86 x 86]
Donated by Mrs Smith
Acc.no.1984-74.1

239. Patchwork / appliqué coverlet

Multi-coloured printed cottons in pink,
mauve, blue, salmon and browns. Reverse
of white cotton. Central white square set
diagonally on mauve printed square within
strip borders made up of squares and
triangles and diamonds. Appliqué patterns
on central square and some borders.
Central patch embroidered in cross-stitch
'Mary Dickinson Thornley 1815'. The
materials were probably specially
purchased for this coverlet. The outer
border may have been a later addition,
c.1820.
1815
Thornley, Co. Durham
295 x 277 (116 x 109)
Donated by Averil Colby
Acc.no.1984-150

240. Embroidered coverlet

Turkey red and white cotton. Reverse of
white cotton. Alternate machine pieced
squares of red and white cotton set around
a central white square embroidered with
monarch's crown, orbs and sceptre ER VII.
Each square bears hand-embroidered name
of chapel member.
1902
Lanchester, Co. Durham
257 x 201 (101 x 79]
Acquired
Acc.no.1984-188

241. Coverlet

Machine pieced coverlet top in Turkey red
and white cotton. No quilting.
c. 1920
Mickleton, Co. Durham
221 x 220 (87 x 87)
Donated by Mr Bates
Acc.no.1985-336.2

242. Walter Scott coverlet

Coverlet of pieced felts, tartans and
suitings. Framed centrepiece intended as
cot coverlet for eldest daughter. Begun in
1870s, but too heavy for use. Enlarged to
full size with machine stitched and pieced
flower shapes. Reverse of cotton sateen.
The material used was off cuts from the
making of suits or coats for farmers and
gentlemen. Made by Walter Scott, a master
tailor.
c. 1870-80
Crookham, Northumberland
213 x 203 (84 x 80)
Acquired
Acc.no.1986-115

243. Hexagon cot cover

Cot coverlet in Turkey red and white
cotton hexagons, with red diamonds and
pyramids. The sides of the hexagons have
been gathered to create a rosette effect.
Outer trim of alternating red and white
pyramids. The coverlet was made by Mrs
Isabella Cruddas.
c.1860-70
125 x 145 (49 x 57)
Rookhope, Weardale
Acquired
Acc.no.1988-315

244. Bible coverlet

Unfinished coverlet consisting of machine
pieced printed cotton texts in monotone
black printing on white cotton. Outer frill
of black printed cotton. Each printed block
is either square or rectangular and a few
are printed with engravings. The coverlet
had been made by chapel members in
Hartlepool.
c. 1880-90
Hartlepool
217 x 214 (85 x 84)
Acquired
Acc.no.1992-76

245. Log cabin coverlet

Multi-coloured wool and tweed fabrics
with plain wool reverse in a "barn raising"
pattern. Beige, brown, orange, navy and
green wools. Made by Katherine
Humphrey.
c. 1930
Wrekenton, Gateshead
175 x 139 (69 x 55)
Anonymous donation
Acc.no.1993-10

246. Poor Law Union signature coverlet

White rectangles of cotton linked with
lace. Each panel has a name embroidered
in pink cable stitch. The larger central
panel is embroidered with 'Darlington
Poor Law Union' and a royal coat of arms.
There is no backing material.
c. 1900-20
Darlington, Co. Durham
244 x 183 (96 x 72)
Acquired
Acc.no.1993-236

247. Turkey red log cabin coverlet

Turkey red and white cotton with white
cotton reverse. Pieced strips forming log
cabin overall diamond pattern. Strong
outer border of pieced strips forming
diamonds. Initialled FS.
c. 1900-10
Weardale, Co. Durham
221 x 201 (87 x 79)
Acquired
Acc.no.1997-75

248. Unfinished pieced coverlet

Early chintz cotton furnishing fabrics in
floral blue, brown and green/yellow.
Border of roller printed blue floral design.
Pieced chintz stars on a white background.
Many of the original paper patterns are still
in place, some from a printed book, some
handwritten dating back to 1748.
c. 1825-35
Berwick upon Tweed, Northumberland
271 x 230 (107 x 91)
Donated by Mrs Linda Brown
Acc.no.2001-10

249. Birtley Victory coverlet

Pink printed and white cotton with no
backing. Pieced pink and white hexagons
embroidered with names of the church
members. Central hexagon embroidered in
yellow 'Oct 1921' and 'Victory Bazaar'
embroidered in green on white cotton,
with 'Birtley PM Church' embroidered in
blue on pink hexagons. The ministers'
names and their dates are also
embroidered. The coverlet completed
fundraising for the purchase of the chapel
building and was made by the ladies of the
Sewing Circle.
1921
Birtley, Co. Durham
210 x 178 (83 x 70)
Donated by Birtley Methodist Church
Acc.no.2002-78

250. Signature coverlet

Primrose cotton strips held together
vertically with open lace work. Reverse
and outer frill of yellow cotton. The strips
are embroidered with names. Possibly a
chapel coverlet.
c. 1890-1900
Otterburn, Northumberland
192 x 166 (75 x 65)
Donated by Mrs Salford
Acc.no.2002-100

251. Framed coverlet

Multicoloured printed cottons, many in
unused condition, a mixture of dress and
furnishing fabrics. Alternating strips and
triangles set around a central square
consisting of eight triangles. Unfinished
with no backing.
1810-1860
Barnard Castle, Co. Durham
261 x 237 (103 x 93)
Acquired
Acc.no.2006-4.2

Further Reading

Allan, Rosemary E.
Quilts and Coverlets from Beamish Museum.
Beamish, The North of England Open Air Museum, 1987

Betterton, Sheila.
Quilts and Coverlets.
The American Museum in Britain.
Bath, 1978

Brears, Peter.
North Country Folk Art.
John Donald, 1989

Chainey, Barbara.
The Essential Quilter.
David and Charles, 1993

Colby, Averil.
Patchwork.
Batsford, 1958

Colby, Averil.
Patchwork Quilts.
Batsford, 1965

Colby, Averil.
Quilting.
Batsford, 1972

Emms, Amy, MBE.
Amy Emms' Story of Durham Quilting.
Search Press, 1990

FitzRandolph, Mavis.
Traditional Quilting.
Batsford, 1954

FitzRandolph, Mavis & Fletcher, Florence.
Quilting.
Dryad Press, 1972

Fox, Sandi.
Wrapped in Glory,
Figurative Quilts and Bedcovers 1700-1900
Thames and Hudson, 1995

Hake, Elizabeth.
English Quilting Old and New.
Batsford, 1937

Nichols, Rachel.
Scripture Coverlets from Printed Blocks.
Quilt Studies.
Journal of the British Quilt Study Group
Issue 6 2004

Osler, Dorothy.
Traditional British Quilts.
Batsford, 1987

Osler, Dorothy.
North Country Quilts: Legend and Living Tradition.
The Bowes Museum and Friends of the Bowes Museum, 2000

Osler, Dorothy.
Across the Pond, New World Influences on Old World Quilt Traditions,
Quilter's Newsletter Magazine No.383 June 2006

Parker, Freda.
Victorian Patchwork.
Anaya, 1991

Quilt Studies Issues 1-8,
The British Quilt Study Group,
The Quilters' Guild,
Halifax, West Yorkshire.

Quilt Treasures:
The Quilters' Guild Heritage Search.
Deirdre McDonald Books, 1995

Rae, Janet.
The Quilts of the British Isles.
Constable, 1987

Seward, Linda.
The Complete Book of Patchwork, Quilting and Appliqué.
Mitchell Beazley, 1987

Sheppard, Josie.
Through the Needle's Eye.
The Patchwork and Quilt Collection at the York Castle Museum.
York Museums Trust, 2005

Stevens, Christine.
Quilts.
National Museum of Wales, 1993

Sykas, Philip A.
The Secret Life of Textiles,
Six Pattern Book Archives in North West England,
Bolton Museums
Bolton 2005

Ward, Anne.
Quilting in the North of England,
Folk Life, vol.4 1966

Acknowledgements

THIS BOOK could not have been written without the collections of Beamish, The North of England Open Air Museum. Over the last 37 years, whilst working at Beamish, I have had the wonderful opportunity, of being able to collect both the information and the quilts themselves. It is a tribute to the many people who have generously donated their quilts and indeed a little bit of their own lives, for future generations to enjoy.

I would like to thank the quilters, whom I have had the privilege of talking to, especially in my early years at Beamish. They gave me an appreciation of the craft, which led to a particular interest in the history of North Country quilting. Amy Emms MBE (1904-1998) encouraged many people to take up the craft and inspired them with her infectious enthusiasm. Amy was never shy of divulging her "secrets" and passed on much of her knowledge to younger generations.

Many of the people who provided me with specialist information on the history of the craft for my first publication, *Quilts and Coverlets from Beamish Museum,* in 1987, are now sadly no longer with us. Mavis FitzRandolph, Florence Fletcher, Averil Colby, Muriel Rose, to name just a few, have helped to preserve knowledge of the crafts of both quilting and patchwork. Their research and information gathering was so important at a time when the tradition was still flourishing. Without their promotion of the craft from 1920-1940, it may well have died out completely. Dorothy Osler has researched North Country quilting tirelessly and has greatly furthered our knowledge through her excellent books on the subject.

Arthur Roberts of Lunedale was an enormous help in locating examples of the craft. He is sadly missed. Mrs.William Sanderson of Hexham kindly provided information on Elizabeth Sanderson. Peter Brears most generously allowed me to use his superb drawings of Beamish quilts. They took hours of painstaking and accurate work, and do give a good understanding of the use of patterns in quilt design. He has been a great source of encouragement over the years.

I am greatly indebted to Justin Battong, for his patience, hard work and superb photography, and for being such fun to work with. Thanks also go to Duncan Davis and Peter Richardson for their photographs. Paul Castrey, in his first job at Beamish, was thrown in at the deep end, to photograph quilts and has taken some excellent details of the fabrics. Special thanks go to Ian C. Brown, for his time and patience. A true perfectionist, he has produced a most sympathetic and imaginative design.

Thanks must go to the museum authorities that have allowed me the opportunity to produce this book. Last of all, and certainly not least, thanks must go to my husband, John Gall, who as Deputy Director at Beamish, has always encouraged and supported me in everything I have done and particularly in this project.

MUSEUMS LIBRARIES ARCHIVES
NORTH EAST

RENAISSANCE
NORTH EAST
museums for
changing lives